21 days to the Perfect Cat

The friendly boot camp for your imperfect pet

Kim Houston

hamlyn

An Hachette UK Company
www.hachette.co.uk

First published in Great Britain in 2014 by
Hamlyn, a division of Octopus Publishing Group Ltd
Endeavour House
189 Shaftesbury Avenue
London
WC2H 8JY
www.octopusbooks.co.uk

Kim Houston asserts the moral right to be identified
as the author of this work

ISBN 978-0-600-62614-5

A CIP catalogue record for this book is available from
the British Library

Printed and bound in China

10 9 8 7 6 5 4 3 2 1

Dedication

'For my gorgeous girl, Gertie.
Although you are sadly gone, your
spirit (and zest for life!) remains in
my heart forever.'

Disclaimer

The advice in this book is provided
as general information only.
It is not necessarily specific to
any individual case and is not a
substitute for the guidance and
advice provided by a licensed
veterinary practitioner consulted in
any particular situation. Octopus
Publishing Group Ltd accepts no
liability or responsibility for any
consequences resulting from the use
of or reliance upon the information
contained herein.

Unless the information given in
this book is specifically for male
cats, cats are referred to throughout
as 'she'. The information is equally
applicable to both male and female
cats, unless otherwise specified.

Contents

Part 1: Introduction

Everything you need to know before starting to train

How to use this book

Whether you have the pleasure of sharing your home with a lively and spirited kitten, a rescue cat, or an older cat, this book is designed to help you get the best from your feline companion. As you may have already discovered, cats are complex individuals with a unique set of needs and requirements. This book will help you to understand those needs by seeing things from the cat's perspective. So whether you are a first-time cat owner, or have been fortunate enough to have cats in your life for many years, there is a wealth of information within these pages that will help you to give your cat a more stimulating, enriched, and fun-filled life.

Introduction

The introduction to this book will give you new insights into your cat's world and a better understanding of her needs and natural behaviours. You will be working with these in the training, guiding her natural behaviours into habits that make both your lives easier and happier. If you have ever wondered whether it is possible to train a cat, the introductory chapters should dispel any doubts that you may have. Positive, kind, and reward-based training techniques will be explained, helping you to train your cat in a structured, happy, and fun way. The introduction concludes with a guide to clicker training, which is a method of training that has long been used for dogs, but will prove to be a valuable tool in training your cat.

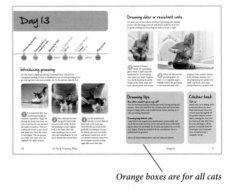

Orange boxes are for all cats

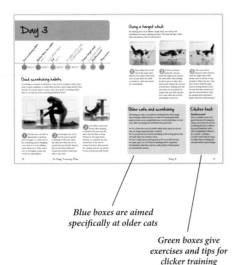

Blue boxes are aimed specifically at older cats

Green boxes give exercises and tips for clicker training

21-Day Training Plan

The main section of the book is a step-by-step training guide aimed at maximizing your cat's potential to become happy and problem-free. You will be guided through a series of daily topics that have been specially selected after many years of listening to cat owners and dealing with hundreds of cat behavioural problems first-hand.

Each day addresses a new subject and provides practical training tasks as well as trouble-shooting tips and advice. The exercises are fun, stimulating, and occasionally challenging. As you work through them, they will enrich your cat's life and strengthen the bond between the two of you.

Timelines

At the top of each day of the plan you will see a colour-coded timeline. This provides a basic structure for the training, by showing how long you and your cat need to spend on each task. You will notice that the timings are marked out in three colours: orange, green, and blue. The timings coloured in orange are for you to attempt with all cats, whether they are young or old, nervous or bold. The timings in green are specifically clicker-training tasks, which can also be attempted by all cats. The timings in blue indicate additional exercises that are specifically designed for older

cats. Exercises shown within boxes on the page are highlighted in grey capitals on the timelines.

Each exercise is allotted a timing on the timelines, but these are purely guidelines – if you have an older, nervous, or timid cat, you may need to shorten the exercise periods. One cat's response to training will invariably differ from another's, so it is important to be guided by your cat. For the best chance of success, make sure that you do everything at your cat's pace.

Quick fixes

The final section contains troubleshooting solutions for 50 problems that are commonly encountered by cat owners, from scratching the furniture to raiding your bin. Problem behaviours are addressed by combining environmental changes, training, and practical management techniques. So, you will find a solution to the problem here.

Most importantly, remember to have fun and to use the time to enhance and strengthen the relationship that you have with your cat. This is the start of your journey to having a happier, well-behaved cat. Good luck!

Kim Houston

Green indicators show clicker tasks for all cats

Orange indicators show tasks for all cats

Some orange indicators show two different timescales: use the shorter time for older cats and the longer time for all other cats

Blue indicators show tasks for older or rescue cats

Colour key for 21-day timelines

For all cats

For older or rescue cats

Clicker tasks for all cats

How to use this book

Through a cat's eyes

Living with cats can be an immensely rewarding and fulfilling experience. Cats are remarkable animals; they are natural-born survivors, great hunters, incredible athletes, loving companions, and intuitive friends. However, they do retain much of the biology and behaviour of their ancestors – wild cats – and it is therefore important to understand their natural behaviours and complex needs.

A cat in the wild would spend her day hunting, feeding, resting, partaking in social activities, and engaging with her environment through exploration and investigation. Contrary to popular belief, the domestic cat is a social animal. Their social system is flexible, allowing cats to live alone or in groups of varying sizes. Cats are masters of communication and transmit information through visual, tactile, olfactory, and auditory means. From the trill and miaow by way of a greeting, to urine-marking or spraying as a part of olfactory communication, these are natural and normal feline behaviours.

A suitable environment

Problems often arise when we superimpose our values and expectations on to our cats. This commonly results in the cat being unable to express her natural feline behaviours due to restrictions in her lifestyle. Modern day-to-day living frequently results in houses designed in a streamlined and minimalist style. In many instances, this reduces the house to its basic necessities, with clean-cut lines, a clutter-free living space and a manicured garden area.

Unfortunately, while this may be aesthetically pleasing to its owner, it is not conducive to a cat's environmental needs. A cat that claws the arm of the leather sofa is often perceived as vindictive and intent on causing trouble. But in fact, this behaviour is perfectly normal; cats need to scratch to keep their claws in good condition and to mark their territory. If the cat is not provided with an alternative outlet for this necessary behaviour, she will use her intellect and find a suitable replacement. Unfortunately, this may be your shiny new leather sofa!

Owners sometimes make the mistake of viewing their cats as solitary individuals who are quintessentially self-reliant. As a result, their cats are often left to their own devices while their human carer is out at work all day. This can lead to boredom and unwanted behaviours.

Natural feline behaviour

In the wild, a cat would have countless trees to scratch and climb, an endless amount of prey to stalk and chase, high-up perches on which to relax in the heat of the sun, and suitable latrines containing soft soil. In other words, nature provides an altogether stimulating and enriched environment. Then, we bring cats into our home to share our space, but often repress many of these natural instincts. Cats are frequently kept in static and monotonous environments with insufficient stimulation and unrealistic rules that can cause or exacerbate behaviour problems. By doing so we are stripping her of her true and fundamental self; in short, we are not allowing her to be a cat!

This creates a conflict between what we view as abnormal and unacceptable behaviour versus natural and instinctual feline behaviour. As a result, the quality of life of both the cat and the owner can suffer. It is important to understand a cat's needs and natural behaviour so that you can modify the environment you provide for her in a way that allows her to redirect her natural instincts into acceptable outlets.

Both indoor and outdoor cats need to be kept physically fit, mentally stimulated, and emotionally satisfied and content. By providing an enriched environment, engaging in play sessions, and providing basic training you can address the needs of you and your cat, creating a harmonious and fulfilling life for you both.

A cat's needs

Environmental enrichment and stimulation is an essential part of providing a safe, fulfilling, and happy home for your cat. Beyond the basic requirements of shelter, food, and water, cats need opportunities to exercise their most natural behaviours in order for them to thrive both mentally and physically. By providing a more stimulating environment and opportunities for scratching, perching, exploration, hunting, and play, you will not only reduce the risk of behavioural problems developing, but will also help to eradicate any existing problems. A dull, uninteresting and understimulating environment can lead to destructive and stress-related behaviours such as chewing household items and overgrooming. Enriching a cat's environment and providing consistency in her routines creates a happier, healthier cat.

The key to enriching the environment is to understand the resources that are particularly valued by the cat and those which will facilitate her natural behaviours. These resources should be provided in abundance and should be incorporated into her daily life and routine. Even if your cat has access to the outdoors, it is still important to enrich her indoor environment, especially if she lives in a multi-cat household. During long, cold winter months for example, she may want to spend more time in the comfort of her home. If provided with the necessary resources she can continue to carry out her natural behaviours indoors without any problem.

Choosing a litter box

Part of creating a healthy environment for your cat involves providing her with a suitable litter box. Whether she is an indoor or outdoor cat, a litter box is an essential resource and should be provided in your house, preferably somewhere private. She may well go outside and explore her environment, but she might not want to toilet there. Cats prefer to toilet in private, and can often be put off toileting outdoors if there are a lot of neighbouring cats. Forcing her outdoors on a cold winter's night can ultimately lead to her secretly toileting in the warmth of the indoors in a suitable hiding place.

Normal feline elimination involves pre-elimination digging, elimination posturing, and post-elimination digging. These natural behaviours must be considered when choosing a suitable litter box. She needs a large open box with enough room to move around. Cats have different preferences but it should contain fine-grained substrate (litter). Being naturally private animals, the position of the litter box requires careful consideration. It should be in a quiet area, free from the hustle and bustle of everyday life. After all, would you like to go to the toilet in full view of the window, or overlooked by friends or family?

Always ensure you position the box away from food and water bowls. Forcing a cat to toilet where she eats and drinks is very unnatural to her and can force her to find an alternative toileting site. If you are lucky enough to share your home with more than one cat, then you must consider the 'litter box ratio'. Competition for resources can lead to stress and anxiety, so be sure to provide each cat with its own litter box, plus one extra. Finally, cats are fastidiously clean animals,

so a thorough litter-tray cleaning regime is vital. If in doubt about whether it needs to be cleaned, just ask yourself, 'Would I toilet in there?'. Help your cat to be as fastidious as she is naturally inclined to be.

Provide a scratching post

Cats need to scratch in order to keep their claws in good condition and to visually mark their territory. Problems arise when the cat chooses to scratch the arm of your new sofa for this purpose, instead of the scratch post you have provided. She is not being vindictive or trying to upset you, she is performing a behaviour that is perfectly normal – it just happens to be in the wrong place! To minimize the risk of this happening and to ensure that her environment provides the 'appropriate' scratching surface, provide a large sisal-covered post, or better still, real bark-covered logs. These provide a surface that she can actually get her claws into and your sofa will be much less attractive to her.

The position of the scratching post is also important. Cats tend to scratch on prominent vertical objects, or scratch after a period of resting. So, if you don't want your cat to scratch your designer furniture when she wakes from having forty winks, provide an alternative scratching place close to where she sleeps.

A preference for height

Climbing to high-up places is a natural behaviour for cats. Not only does it allow them to feel safe and secure, it also gives them the opportunity to survey their territory and engage in opportunistic hunting. High surfaces provide both mental and physical stimulation and keep cats entertained. However, human beings live largely in a horizontal world and our homes are often not conducive to our cat's vertical needs. This means you will probably need to make a deliberate effort to provide unrestricted access to resting areas at varying heights. These vertical spaces will add to your cat's security and reduce tension in multi-cat households. They also provide escape routes during challenging times, such as over-exuberant children, a buoyant puppy, or scary noises such as the vacuum cleaner. You can create a cat-friendly, vertical environment in many ways: simply providing a bed on top of a cupboard, investing in a multi-perch cat tree, or, if you are adventurous, by constructing a cat walkway high up on your walls – she will love you for this!

Happy feeding arrangements

Cats are natural hunters and in the wild will spend many solitary hours of their day looking for and capturing small prey. Problems arise in day-to-day living when owners 'force' cats to eat next to one another. This is unnatural to cats and will increase tension and competition in a multi-cat household. Each cat requires her own food and water station, in a quiet area and out of view of the other cats.

Out of kindness, owners often provide their cats with an abundance of 'free' food, but given the opportunity, cats usually prefer to express their predatory instincts and hunt for their food. You can accommodate her natural eating habits by making her work for her food (see pages 48–49). Mealtimes can and should be mentally and physically stimulating, so try offering her some of her daily ration in a feeding ball or other device that is specifically designed to release dry food. Forms of 'activity feeding' mean that she will have to use her senses, skills, and mental dexterity to work out how to get the food, and resemble more closely her situation in the wild.

Social interaction with people

There is a popular misconception that cats are aloof, standoffish, and unsociable when it comes to human contact. The truth of the matter is that our cats benefit hugely from predictable and consistent interaction with humans, either through play, grooming, or a cuddle session! However, depending on their genetics and socialization, the amount of contact that cats require varies enormously. If a cat has experienced positive handling in her early life (3–7 weeks of age), then she should grow up accepting cuddles from her human family. But if she has not been adequately socialized, she may tolerate much less human contact.

As a rule of thumb, most cats prefer to be in control of the amount of contact they receive, and ordinarily this would be low-intensity but frequent contact. So respect her boundaries and space and take things at her pace. Never force her to be handled, as this leads to stress and anxiety, and the next time you approach her, she will run away. In fact, you will probably find that it is the visitor who shows the least interest in your cat that will be most frequently pestered for attention!

Consistency and routine

Although structure and routine can sometimes seem very boring to us, for animals it is vital as consistency minimizes stress. Cats are creatures of habit, and have great internal clocks. You only have to recall how they appear on cue for their breakfast every day!

Changes to a cat's routine can lead to stress and anxiety, and even the development of behavioural problems. Some of the most important routines to structure into your cat's day include scheduled play sessions, regular mealtimes, and predictable contact and grooming sessions. Once you've established a routine that suits both you and your cat, try to stick to the schedule as much as possible, as she will look forward to her daily activities. What may only be five minutes out of your day is very important in her little world.

Finally, a word of warning: be careful of the routine you develop. If you get up at 6am to feed her on weekdays, she will expect to be fed at 6 a.m. at the weekends too! Plan a routine that is realistic and achievable every day, and that suits you both well.

Outlets for play

Providing appropriate outlets for play is essential in putting together an environmental enrichment programme. Sadly, this fundamental area is often neglected by cat owners, even though play is one of the secret weapons in the key to a happy cat. We think it is so important that it deserves a section of its own.

Daily play sessions

One of the most effective ways to provide the mental and physical stimulation that your cat needs is to schedule daily, interactive play sessions with her. Cats have an innate desire to hunt, so play should closely resemble the natural predatory sequence of stalking, chasing, pouncing, and biting. Play is an essential activity for cats of all ages, young and old, and not only does it encourage bonding between you, it also prevents boredom, reduces anxiety, and is a great form of exercise. We have to respect that cats are athletic creatures with incredible stamina, both mentally and physically, and play gives them a natural outlet for this energy and satisfies their prey drive.

Stimulating toys

All cats require a selection of toys to cover their instinctive needs: some toys are better for chasing, some for pouncing on, some to bat around, and some are ideal to hunt. Cats have their own unique set of needs when it comes to play. Some cats prefer to engage in ground hunting games, such as chasing a ball across the floor, while other cats prefer aerial pursuits. You may have tried to cater for your cat's every play desire, and provided an entire toy box packed full of toys. However, to your cat these static toys are essentially dead prey, as they don't move, and your cat may see them as boring.

Some of the most enjoyable and fulfilling toys for cats are 'interactive' toys. These create the most intense and satisfying play sessions, often sending

her into a complete frenzy! Interactive toys are those that are controlled by you, usually using a fishing rod with an interchangeable attachment. You can then make the 'prey' move in a lifelike manner, by making it wriggle, creep, fly, or dart, just like real prey. This will provide her with an outlet for her hunting behaviour and it's great exercise and a source of stress relief too.

Key points for fun-filled play
There are four key things to remember when using toys to play with your cat:
● **Move the toy to resemble prey**
This will trigger your cat's prey drive. Don't wave a toy around frantically or move it directly in front of her – she knows that this is not the way prey behaves! Instead, subtly quiver the toy to get her attention and then alternate between fast and slow movements; a bird or a mouse would not normally move in a constant predictable manner.
● **Don't touch your cat with the toy**
Remember, you are trying to simulate 'real' prey and it is very unlikely in the cat's natural habitat that a rodent would actually walk up to a cat.

Move the toy away from your cat and hide it behind a piece of furniture. Continue until she stalks, follows, and eventually pounces on the toy.
● **Allow your cat to taste success**
Your cat needs to have several 'captures' of the toy so that she doesn't become frustrated. Give her the opportunity to swat the toy with her paw and then allow her to pounce on it as she would in the wild. These victories will serve to build her confidence.
● **Always end on a positive note**
End the play session by giving your cat a few tasty treats. After all, this is what would happen in the wild; she would stalk, chase, ambush, kill, and then eat her prey! Giving a tasty morsel will signify the end of the game and also help your cat to feel accomplished and victorious.

> Maintain a regular schedule of interactive play, so that your cat has consistency. As a guideline, schedule two 10-minute sessions daily from Day 1 of the 21-Day Plan.

Can I train a cat?

Contrary to popular belief, cats can be trained and are intellectually one of the smartest of all companion animals. The intelligence of an adult cat is often compared to that of a three-year-old child, and we know how clever (and crafty) a small child can be. Is it any wonder that cats are better at training their owners than the owners are at training them? Does your cat paw you gently on the face until you give her space in your bed? Or does she rouse you in the middle of the night for food? Succumbing to feeding your cat when she miaows at 3am means you are inadvertently reinforcing this behaviour. Cats will soon learn that miaowing is rewarded with food and you'll never have another peaceful night!

When it comes to training animals, most people think of dogs. Dogs are acclaimed for their obedience and willingness to learn, while cats are often incorrectly viewed as stubborn, defiant, and untrainable. Cats may not respond to training in the same way as a dog, but they hold as much ability to be trained. Training is about understanding the animal and appreciating their motivations. Dogs love to please their owners but cats like to please themselves!

Understanding your cat

By taking time to understand your cat, and by tapping into her natural behaviour, it is possible to successfully train her. Cats are surprisingly fast learners once we humans figure out what motivates them. By expanding on natural cat behaviours it is possible to train basic commands such as 'stay' or to teach cats to perform certain tasks, such as how to use a cat flap. Training your cat can also lead to improved compliance during

Introduction

daily tasks such as grooming, handling, and health checks. It is also good for your cat's mental and physical wellbeing, and will strengthen the bond between you and your cat.

What you should know

The two principal considerations when training your cat are, firstly, looking at her natural behaviours and motivations and, secondly, employing positive, kind, and reward-based training methods. The most important lesson for you, the owner, is *never* to punish your cat, whether in the context of training or otherwise. Punishment does not work and has no place in any interactions we have with our cats. Aversive and punitive techniques not only lead to fear and anxiety, but harsh reprimands also slow down the learning process.

In addition, confrontational behaviour will undoubtedly damage the trusting relationship that your cat has with you. On one hand you are the provider of all that's good in her world, but at other times, through her eyes, you are unpredictable and unkind for no obvious reason. Training needs to be positive, kind, and above all else, fun. As a trainer, you will need lots of patience and understanding if your cat is to succeed with her tasks. Whatever the aim of the training, it needs to be done at her pace and can therefore be a time-consuming but rewarding process. The fundamental underpinning of training is to reward the desired behaviour instantly. Therefore, the only outcome for your cat is reward and success, an altogether positive training experience.

Reward-based training

The reward that you use during training sessions must be of 'high value' in order to keep her concentration and give her an incentive to work. Therefore you must determine your cat's favourite reward (even if it is select cuts of prime salmon) and use this. Dogs will usually respond to any kind of treat, irrespective of value, and they will work for them even when they are not particularly hungry. However, everyday cat biscuits are very unlikely to hold your cat's attention and you will probably find that she walks away and ignores you. Cats can be hard to please and indifferent to praise for doing something well, so as the trainer, you too will be working hard. A good tip to bear in mind before you start your training is to make sure that your cat is hungry and interested.

Clicker training

Clicker training is a training technique often seen in the dog world, but its origins date back over 30 years when many of the principles were used to train marine mammals. Today, although it is far more popular in dog training, the same principles can also be used to train our feline friends.

Positive reinforcement

Clicker training is a positive training experience for any animal; it uses food as the primary tool of reinforcement, involves no punishment, and utilizes short, regular training sessions. If implemented correctly, animals not only enjoy the learning experience but progress through it very quickly with impressive results. All training needs to be positive and fun, with an emphasis on clear signals and excellent timing of rewards. By using a clicker these fundamental key areas are more readily achievable.

How does clicker training work?

A clicker is a small plastic device with a metal strip that makes a clicking sound when pressed. The clicker noise is a very distinctive and consistent sound within your cat's environment, and it is very unlikely that anything in her world emits the same noise. In effect, the clicker creates an efficient language between you and your cat and becomes a clear form of communication. The idea behind clicker training is that the click serves as

a 'bridge' between the desired behaviour and the cat's reward. Put simply, when your cat performs a desired behaviour, you click immediately and then reward her for her efforts by giving her a tasty treat. She will quickly learn that when she hears this noise it means that she has done something desirable, and that the sound of the click means that a tasty food reward will follow soon afterwards. Although the human voice can be used instead, the clicker is a much faster, simpler, and more effective means of communicating that your cat has performed the correct behaviour.

The click also makes it easier to mark the 'exact' behaviour that you require. Animals live in the present and, to make learning more effective, we need to let them know immediately that they have performed the desired behaviour.

'Charging the clicker'

The first step is to get your cat used to the sound of the clicker and teach her to associate the sound of the click with a reward. This process is known as 'charging the clicker'. Remember, for the best chance of success it is important to choose an extra-special food reward and indulge her with

her favourite delicacy. It is often better to use a soft food reward such as chicken, as this is easier and quicker for your cat to eat; biscuits will take her too long to chew, and she may lose the association with the behaviour and the reward.

When you have found a food item that you think will motivate her, cut it up into tiny bite-size pieces. When deciding on the treat size, consider that for a medium-sized dog (such as a Labrador), an appropriate-sized reward would be the size of a pea. This allows some appreciation of just how small your cat's treats should be! Although she will be working hard for the rewards, you don't want her to gain any unnecessary weight in the process. Remember too that food is not necessarily the only reinforcing tool that can be used in training – you can use anything that motivates her to work. However, most cats would prefer to receive a tasty morsel of salmon or ham, rather than praise or a toy, and who can blame them!

To begin with, take a few treats in your hand and sit on the floor with your cat. Click the clicker and then toss her a treat. She does not have to perform any particular behaviour here; you just want her to associate the sound of the clicker with

an immediate and very tasty reward. Some cats will achieve this almost immediately, while others may take a little longer to figure it out. Be patient and don't rush her. If your cat looks uninterested or seems to walk away in disdain, do not give up. The reward you have chosen is probably not motivating enough, or she is simply not hungry. Either try a different reward or wait until your cat is hungry. Training should never last for more than a few minutes at a time and should always finish on a good note. Once your cat readily makes an association between the sound of the click and the reward, you can start to introduce some training exercises and more advanced clicker techniques.

Three routes to clicker training

To train your cat to perform a desired behaviour using a clicker you can either use 'capturing', 'shaping', or 'luring'. Each of these clicker training techniques has its own unique benefits, but they can all be used in conjunction with each other. With time and patience you can teach your cat any behaviour with these methods, whether training her to enter her cat carrier, or training her to perform simple tricks such as 'sit' or 'shake a paw'. Do not be put off by the word 'trick' – this is not

meant to demean your cat in any way. It is merely taking some of her natural and basic movements and modifying them (with the help of positive reinforcement) until she can perform a slightly different behaviour. Whatever clicker task you choose, its aim is to improve your cat's daily life by providing her with stimulation and enriching her environment.

'Capturing' a behaviour

'Capturing' involves choosing a behaviour your cat does naturally, such as sitting, lying down, or rolling on the grass, and then playing a waiting-and-watching game until she performs the desired behaviour. For instance, when she decides to lie down of her own accord, the moment her body touches the ground, click and then toss her a tasty treat. She will then have to get up out of the lying position to retrieve her reward. At this early stage she won't have a clue as to why she's earned a tasty tidbit, but after several repetitions she will hopefully form an association between lying down and receiving her reward. This training technique can take a lot of time and patience before she forms the association and performs the behaviour on command.

'Shaping' a behaviour

Alternatively, if you would like to teach your cat a new behaviour such as raising a paw, you can achieve this by 'shaping' her behaviour. Shaping involves breaking down a complex behaviour into tiny steps and rewarding her for each small successive movement she makes towards reaching the final goal: the desired behaviour.

To get your cat to raise a paw you might start by clicking when she shifts her weight off one of her paws slightly, repeating this several times. Then delay the click until she lifts her paw off the ground slightly before rewarding her. Next, delay the click until she raises her paw a little higher, and once again click then treat. In essence, what you are trying to do is reinforce the tiny steps she makes until she reaches the ultimate goal.

'Luring' with treats

'Luring' involves using a treat or a 'target stick' (see page 31) to guide your cat into the desired position. For example, if you want to lure your cat into a sitting position, take a tasty treat (the 'lure') and hold it just above (but slightly behind) her head. As she reaches backwards towards the treat, her bottom will naturally hit the floor. Click then treat to reward her behaviour.

Cue words

Whether you use capturing, shaping, or luring, when you feel she has made the connection between the behaviour and the click–treat, you can then give that behaviour a name, otherwise known as a 'cue' word. This should be a short, unique word that is easy to say, easily remembered, and that describes the desired behaviour. Examples include 'sit', 'stay', or 'bed'.

For instance, if you have been rewarding your cat for 'staying' in a particular place, now you would simply add the cue word (or hand signal) 'stay'. Ideally, you want her to relate the word 'stay' to the desired behaviour of staying. Don't assume that she will instantly associate the cue with the behaviour; this requires lots of repetitions before she will reliably perform the behaviour on cue. Be patient and give her the time she needs to perfect these new skills.

21-Day Training Plan

This programme includes a variety of clicker-training tasks incorporating capturing, shaping, and luring. If you are feeling adventurous, you could widen clicker training by using it on some of the other exercises too. Always keep it positive and, above all, remember to have fun!

Being prepared

This introductory section has given you a lot of theoretical knowledge about how your cat sees the world and what you as an owner need to provide to help her develop into a happy, content, and well-behaved cat. Now you need to put that knowledge into practice as you work through the 21-Day Training Plan.

Before you begin the training exercises, it is a good idea to establish whether you have set up your cat's basic environment properly and to check that she has the necessary resources that she will require. Secondly, it's very important that you are well prepared for the training days and that you have the correct tools and training equipment to hand. There is nothing more frustrating than starting a training session and having to stop half-way through because you realize that you are missing some of the essential equipment.

Checklist

Use the checklist opposite to ensure that your cat has got a suitably enriched environment, as outlined in the rest of this introductory section. Providing these resources is the first step to a happy, content, and stimulated cat. The checklist is intended as a guide to items that you will need; some of these you are likely to have already, others are less common and you may need to buy or borrow them before you start the exercises in which they are used. For equipment that will become part of your cat's everyday environment – such as litter boxes, scratching posts, and feeding areas – remember to pay particular attention to where you decided to place them.

Ready to start!

So, now that you have a cat, all her essential resources and equipment, and this training plan, it's time to begin! Please note that on certain days, you may have to enlist the help of a friend or relative for some of the exercises – look through the plan in advance to see where this applies. Where at all possible, it's recommended that you follow the plan day-by-day, keeping the exercises in sequence. However, if you do have to miss a day (we all have busy lives!), then simply pick up where you left off. Some cats may find it difficult to grasp some of the concepts in the training days; if this happens with your cat, don't give up – simply repeat the task until she becomes proficient. Remember, the key to a good training session is patience, consistency, and above all else, fun. I hope you enjoy the journey.

Introduction

Resources and environmental needs

Litter boxes

Single-cat household:
- [ ] Large open litter box (hood removed)
- [ ] 2–3 inches of fine-grained substrate
- [ ] Positioned in private and quiet area
- [ ] Away from food and water bowls
- [ ] Away from noisy household appliances

Multi-cat household: (in addition to above)
- [ ] 1 litter box per cat, plus 1 extra
- [ ] Different locations

Scratching posts

Single-cat household:
- [ ] Large, sturdy, vertical scratching post
- [ ] Sisal-covered commercial post, or bark-covered log
- [ ] Placed in a prominent position in a room where your cat spends much of her time, and close to where she sleeps

Multi-cat household: (in addition to above)
- [ ] 1 scratching post per cat
- [ ] Placed in different locations

Vertical spaces

Single-cat household:
- [ ] Several high-up resting places
- [ ] Positioned in a sunny area with an outside view

Multi-cat household (in addition to above):
- [ ] Individual resting places
- [ ] Placed in different locations

Toys
- [ ] Interactive toys: wand or fishing rod toy
- [ ] Stand-alone toys to bat around, such as pretend mice, small balls

Clicker training
- [ ] Clicker
- [ ] Target stick (or alternative, such as chopstick)
- [ ] Tasty treats, such as chicken (chopped into tiny pieces)

Grooming
- [ ] Grooming brush
- [ ] Grooming glove
- [ ] Pet-formula toothpaste
- [ ] Nail clippers

Other items
- [ ] Harness and leash/cat-walking jacket
- [ ] Break-away safety collar
- [ ] Cat carrier
- [ ] Catnip leaves or spray

Optional items
- [ ] Cat trees and cat walkways

Part 2:
21-Day Training Plan

Your step-by-step guide to complete cat training

Day 1

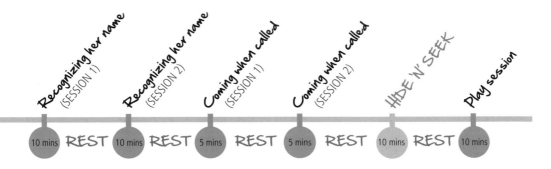

Recognizing her name (SESSION 1)
10 mins · REST

Recognizing her name (SESSION 2)
10 mins · REST

Coming when called (SESSION 1)
5 mins · REST

Coming when called (SESSION 2)
5 mins · REST

HIDE 'N' SEEK
10 mins · REST

Play session
10 mins

Recognizing her name

Teaching your cat to recognize her name is one of the most essential skills she can learn. It means you can get her attention even when she is being drawn into unpleasant or dangerous situations, and enables her to learn to come when called (see opposite).

1 When your cat is near you, softly call her name; if she looks towards you, reward her with a treat. If she begins to look at you in anticipation of a treat, praise and reward her instantly. Reward any attempts she makes to turn her head towards you in response to hearing her name.

2 Say her name over and over again as you give her one of her favourite tidbits. Similarly, when you prepare her meal, hand-feed her a small amount, while saying her name softly. Repeat this exercise several times a day, but keep the sessions brief.

3 In the evening, when she is resting on your lap, gently stroke her while repeating her name in a calm voice. She will quickly associate the sound of her name with a positive and pleasant response from you.

Coming when called

Training your cat to come when called is fun and practical – you'll be able to call her to feed or play at a time to suit you. Aim for at least two training sessions a day, of about 5 minutes each.

1 Stand a little distance away from your cat and call her by name. When she comes, reward her immediately. Once your cat recognizes the association between her name and something pleasurable, you can move on to step 2.

2 Try calling your cat from another room; eventually she will come running even when you're out of sight. When she does, reward her straight away with a treat or play.

3 Continue to practise this exercise until your cat is coming on your first call. Then give her more space and distractions to contend with. Start to reward only her fastest responses, to increase her skill.

Hide 'n' seek

For older cats who readily respond to their name, try challenging them by having a game of hide 'n' seek.

Start by hiding (somewhere easy at first), and then call your cat. Whenever she finds you, give her a big reward. Make the game more difficult by hiding in obscure places!

Name training tips

● While name training, arm yourself with extra tasty treats for your cat, such as pieces of chicken. Cats are seldom motivated if all you offer them is their regular biscuits.
● When calling your cat, refrain from using cute nicknames. Use one name only and stick with it.
● Don't try calling your cat when she's asleep or distracted by something else. Initially, only call her when she is looking at you.
● Ensure the rest of the family is familiar with your training methods and that they use the commands consistently.
● Never call your cat to you for something unpleasant, such as to take medication – she will learn not to respond to her name.

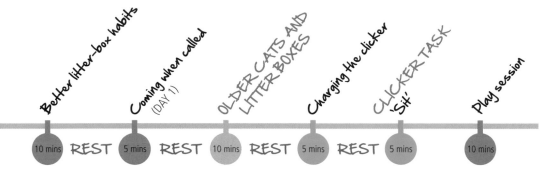

Day 2

Better litter-box habits | Coming when called (DAY 1) | OLDER CATS AND LITTER BOXES | Charging the clicker | CLICKER TASK 'Sit' | Play session

10 mins — REST — 5 mins — REST — 10 mins — REST — 5 mins — REST — 5 mins — 10 mins

Better litter-box habits

Cats are naturally very clean animals and are usually trained by their mothers early in life. However, some youngsters miss out on this training or may need extra help and encouragement to develop good litter-box habits.

1 Place the litter box in a quiet and private area, and fill with a few inches of soft, fine-grained litter. Take your cat to the litter box so she knows where it is and gently place her inside. She may not do anything, but reward her for being there.

2 While there, gently move her front paws in a scratching and digging motion. She will soon get the idea. Repeat this often during the day, particularly after feeding, sleeping, or playing. Speak to her in a praising, soft voice.

3 If she begins to sniff the litter, back away to give her privacy. During the day, watch for signs, such as scratching or sniffing, that might indicate she needs to toilet and place her in the box. Never force her into the box or punish 'accidents'.

Charging the clicker

When your cat learns to associate the sound of a clicker with a reward, the clicker becomes a useful training tool. Learning this association is known as 'charging the clicker'.

1 Pick up a tiny piece of your cat's favourite treat and give it to her while simultaneously clicking (just one click!). You can give her the treat either by handing it to her or tossing it to the floor. She will learn quickly that a click means an immediate reward.

2 Keep repeating the exercise and make sure you do not talk to or touch her. Then move on to clicking first, and giving her the treat a second later. Click then treat! Do not repeatedly click, or hold the clicker close to her.

Clicker task

'Sit'

To teach your cat a simple task, such as 'sit', crouch down and hold a treat just above her head. As she reaches backwards she will naturally sit – immediately click and reward her with the treat. Repeat several times, and then add the cue word 'sit' as she naturally does so.

Older cats and litter boxes

Older cats, or those from a rescue home, can develop an aversion to their litter box for many reasons. Retraining inappropriate toileting habits involves first identifying the problem, then reinforcing new routines, and it requires plenty of patience.

● Initially, try putting several litter boxes in private locations, and remove any hoods. If you have several cats, provide one litter box per cat, plus one extra. Use different substrates in each box, such as potting soil, sand and fine-grained litter. Cats are exceptionally clean, so ensure you have a fastidious cleaning regime for all litter boxes.
● Speaking softly, show your cat the litter boxes and reward any positive steps towards them, then apply steps 1 to 3 of 'Better litter-box habits' (opposite). Be sure to avoid all punishment as this will only reinforce any unwanted behaviour.

Day 3

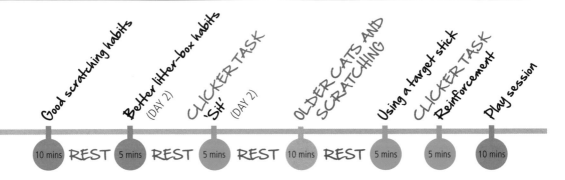

Good scratching habits

Better litter-box habits (DAY 2)

CLICKER TASK 'Sit' (DAY 2)

OLDER CATS AND SCRATCHING

Using a target stick

CLICKER TASK Reinforcement

Play session

10 mins   REST   5 mins   REST   5 mins   REST   10 mins   REST   5 mins   5 mins   10 mins

Good scratching habits

Scratching is a normal cat behaviour. Cats need to scratch to keep their claws in good condition, to mark their territory, and to help stretch their muscles. It is much easier to train a new cat in good scratching habits than it is to stop her from scratching forbidden items.

1 Provide your cat with an appropriate scratching post (see page 11). Entice her to the scratching post by dangling a toy close to it or by rubbing some catnip on it. If she comes over to investigate, praise and reward her immediately.

2 Encourage your cat to use the post by gently scratching it with your nails; this often provokes the cat to scratch the post herself. Repeat this several times daily and reward any positive behaviour with a tasty treat.

3 Cats often scratch and stretch after sleeping, so position the post near the place that she likes to sleep. Whenever she approaches, touches, or scratches the post, reward her. If she tries to scratch furniture, don't punish her: simply pick her up, put her by the scratch post and reward.

21-Day Training Plan

Using a target stick

By training your cat to follow a target stick, you will lay the foundation for many training exercises. This task will take a little time and patience, but it's well worth it.

1 Rub a little food on the end of the target stick. Hold it a few inches away from your cat and when she sniffs or touches it, click and reward her immediately.

2 If your cat doesn't grasp the concept, move the target stick towards her nose rather than waiting for her to go to it, then click and reward. Repeat the exercise several times, making sure that each time you re-present the target stick, you click and give her a treat when she actively participates in any way.

3 Once your cat has learned to show interest, move the target stick a little further away so she has to step towards it. When she does, click then reward. Hold the target stick at varying distances from her and click then reward each time her nose touches it. Keep the sessions short and always finish while she is still interested.

Older cats and scratching

Retraining an older cat in good scratching habits takes longer than training a kitten because it's easier to initiate good habit patterns than correct undesirable ones. Use the tips below to help your older cat change her bad habits into good ones.

- Use a deterrent (such as double-sided sticky tape) on objects that are being inappropriately scratched.
- Do not punish your cat for scratching in the wrong places; this will only make the situation worse.
- Place a large sisal scratching post in the most affected area.
- Apply steps 1 to 3 of 'Good scratching habits' (opposite).
- Remember that time, patience, and positive reinforcement are essential for success.

Clicker task

Reinforcement
Start to reinforce your cat's good behaviour by using the clicker. Each time you see her scratching the post, reinforce this good behaviour with a 'click' immediately, followed by a reward – timing is crucial! It won't take her long to realize that scratching the new post leads to good things.

Day 4

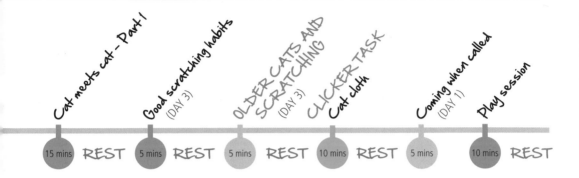

Cat meets cat – Part 1 | 15 mins | REST
Good scratching habits (DAY 3) | 5 mins | REST
OLDER CATS AND SCRATCHING (DAY 3) | 5 mins | REST
CLICKER TASK Cat cloth | 10 mins | REST
Coming when called (DAY 1) | 5 mins
Play session | 10 mins | REST

New cat, old cat

Incorrect introductions are one of the main reasons that multi-cat households encounter problems. Poor introductions can often lead to friction and tension between the cats which can prove difficult to resolve without professional help. The instructions and tips given over the next few pages will ensure a more harmonious connection between your cats.

Slowly does it...

Contrary to common belief, cats are not solitary animals and many enjoy company and benefit from having a feline friend. However, cats are naturally territorial, so introductions to other cats need to be handled slowly and carefully. If you rush this process, or simply throw them together, you will end up with unhappy cats. Not only can this lead to an ongoing war between them, but they may also develop behavioural problems which can prove difficult to rectify.

In order to achieve harmony from the beginning and promote a lifelong friendship between your cats, make the introductions over time and always at your old cat's pace. By using the series of structured exercises in 'Cat meets cat' (see pages 33 and 36–37) and lots of positive reinforcement, you can achieve a stress-free home and your cats will be happy.

Clicker task

Cat cloth

You can use a clicker as part of the introduction process to strengthen any positive associations. The best way to do this is to click and reward any positive moves that the cats make towards each other's cloths (see below). For example, when either cat walks towards or sniffs the other's cloth, click then reward by tossing a treat. Impeccable timing is crucial, so be ready with your clicker. If either cat plays or sleeps near the other cat's cloth, or shows no negative reaction, then click and reward. Any behaviour that isn't negative is positive, so should be reinforced immediately.

Cat meets cat – Part 1

Set up a 'sanctuary' room for your new cat to live in when she first arrives. Make sure this has a solid door and some hiding places, and provide her with all that she needs: a litter box, food and water stations, a bed, and some toys. When you place her in this room, do not let your other cat (or cats) see her or come into contact with her.

1 Once your new cat is settled, you need to get the cats to accept each other's scent. This can be achieved by exchanging facial pheromones. Take a soft cloth or sock, and gently rub it around the new cat's chin and mouth. The idea is to harvest pheromones from her scent glands.

2 Take the cloth to your other cat's area. Do not force her to sniff the cloth; simply place it near her and allow her to investigate. Reward any advances she makes towards the cloth with a treat. If she doesn't show any negative behaviour, praise and reward.

3 Repeat steps 1 and 2 on the second cat, collecting its pheromones on a cloth and delivering it to your new cat. Reward any positive, calm behaviour shown by the new cat and repeat the exercise once a day for several days. Once the cats are calm, proceed to Part 2 (see page 36).

Day 5

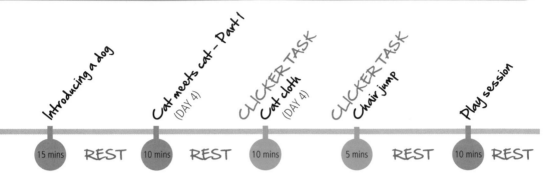

Introducing a dog | Cat meets cat – Part I (DAY 4) | CLICKER TASK Cat cloth (DAY 4) | CLICKER TASK Chair jump | Play session

15 mins   REST   10 mins   REST   10 mins   5 mins   REST   10 mins   REST

Introducing a dog

Cats and dogs can become great companions, but it is crucial that their first meeting is handled patiently and with care.

1 Place your dog in his favourite spot, and your cat in her sanctuary room, allowing her time to settle. As she relaxes, exchange scents between your cat and dog. This helps them to become familiar with each other's smell. Reward all positive behaviour.

2 If step 1 goes well, swap their rooms for a short while without letting them come into contact. They will pick up and transfer scents in each other's area. Reward throughout and then put them back in their respective rooms.

3 To allow safe and controlled introductions, assemble a baby-gate at the doorway of your cat's room. Attach your dog to a leash and sit him away from the gate, rewarding him when he focuses on you and not the cat. If either animal appears stressed, move them away from the gate. Repeat the exercise, gradually moving the dog closer.

Clicker task

Chair jump

Once your cat has mastered following a target stick (see page 31), it's time for the next stage – getting her to jump onto a chair!

Get her to focus on the target stick and when she touches it, click and reward. Next, guide the target stick onto the chair. Click and reward any advances she makes towards the target. If she stretches towards it, or jumps onto the chair to touch it, click then treat instantaneously. Practise this exercise over several days.

Tips for happy cats and dogs

- If you have to leave the house during the introductory period, keep the animals in their respective areas.
- Leave the baby-gate in place for a few weeks so that your cat will always have her own safe area.
- Feed your cat on a high surface that your dog cannot reach; it will help her to feel secure.
- Provide your cat with plenty of escape routes in case she becomes anxious.
- Keep her litter box in the sanctuary room and keep this space dog-free.
- Do not rush the exercises – good introductions take time.

4 Walk your dog in front of the gate and reward any calm behaviour. If the dog lunges towards the gate, don't punish him, just walk him away then try again. He will soon learn that calm behaviour will earn him a treat. Practise this exercise over a few days.

5 When your cat and dog are both consistently calm and relaxed, try feeding them together at a distance from either side of the gate. Keep your dog on a leash and reward any good behaviour from either animal.

6 When your cat and dog seem happy in each other's presence, allow them to walk freely around the house, but always under supervision. Keep your dog's leash attached (trailing, so you can stand on it) until he is unconcerned by your cat's presence.

Day 6

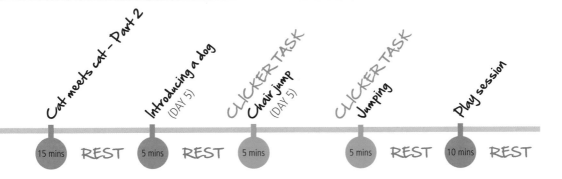

Cat meets cat - Part 2 · Introducing a dog (DAY 5) · CLICKER TASK Chair jump (DAY 5) · CLICKER TASK Jumping · Play session

15 mins · REST · 5 mins · REST · 5 mins · 5 mins · REST · 10 mins · REST

Cat meets cat - Part 2

Once the exchange of scent between your cats has taken place, and each cat seems happy in the presence of the other's scent, you can start to think about bringing them into closer contact with one another. As long as this is done slowly, your cats should develop a good relationship.

1 Having established a communal scent between your cats, you can move on to putting the cats into each other's rooms, without allowing them to come into contact with each other. Be sure to reward calm behaviour before returning them to their original rooms.

2 Next, you need to help them associate each other's presence with something pleasurable, such as food. Place two bowls of your cats' favourite food at equal distance on either side of the closed sanctuary door. Gradually move the bowls closer to the door if the cats seem relaxed.

3 When the cats are comfortable eating at the closed door, try opening it a few inches and secure with a doorstop. Repeat this exercise several times during the day with small portions of tasty food. Even if the process seems to be taking a while, it is important not to rush it.

21-Day Training Plan

Tips for friendship success

- Training sessions will take time and patience, so don't rush them; everything should be at your cats' pace to ensure they remain relaxed.
- If you see any negative body language, such as tail-swishing, flattened ears, or hissing, go back a few steps.
- To reduce competition, provide enough resources for all cats, especially hiding places and high-up resting places.
- Always give your cats separate feeding and water stations.
- Always have one litter box per cat, plus one extra.
- Have regular interactive play sessions.
- Be sure to supervise all interactions.

Clicker task

Jumping

Continue your target training by playing this simple jumping game with your cat. Put a few chairs in a line, then use your target stick to get your cat to jump onto the first chair. Click then treat. Move the target stick to the next chair in line and repeat, rewarding all positive moves with a click and treat. Soon she will jump from chair to chair.

4 Now you can replace the sanctuary door with a mesh door (or screen) so the cats can see each other. Again, place food at a comfortable distance from the door and gradually move the bowls closer. Take things slowly, working at a pace that appears to be comfortable for the cats.

5 Instigate a play session by using a double-ended cat toy. Place the toy through the door, so one part is in the sanctuary room and the second part is with your other cat. Encourage play by using a little catnip.

6 If both cats look relaxed during the mutual eating and play, the final stage is to allow them to interact without any barriers. If the cats show any anxiety or aggression, you must separate them immediately and go back a few steps.

Day 7

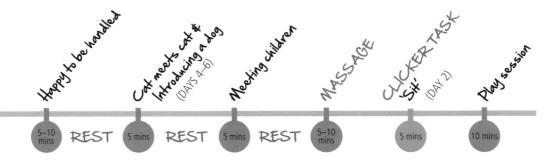

Happy to be handled		Cat meets cat & Introducing a dog (DAYS 4–6)		Meeting children		MASSAGE	CLICKER TASK 'Sit' (DAY 2)	Play session

5–10 mins | REST | 5 mins | REST | 5 mins | REST | 5–10 mins | 5 mins | 10 mins

Happy to be handled

The following training exercises will teach your cat to tolerate being touched and handled. The earlier you expose her to these experiences, the easier it will be to cuddle, groom, transport, and medicate her. Younger cats can practise for 10 minutes; limit older cats to 5 minutes.

1 Begin when your cat is relaxed and content. Initially, you are aiming for her to accept being touched. Gently stroke the top of her head or at the base of her tail – cats usually find it pleasurable being stroked in these areas – but avoid touching her tummy or paws. Reward and praise.

2 Slowly work up to touching other areas of her body, rewarding her throughout. Keep the sessions brief and ensure all handling is pleasurable and positive. Don't rush the exercises; everything should be at your cat's pace. If she tries to escape, let her; do not restrain her.

3 The next step is to briefly pick her up. Gently lift her from the ground. You want her to feel supported, not restrained. Hold her for a few seconds and then put her down again. Reward, praise, and repeat. If she seems happy, gradually increase the duration.

Meeting children

Children love to stroke and handle cats, but unless a cat is used to being handled, this may be frightening for her. It is therefore imperative to supervise any interaction between cat and child.

1 Cats may be more nervous of interactions with children, who are lively and, to a cat, unpredictable. Start off slowly by asking your child to sit quietly on the floor, avoiding sudden movements. When the cat approaches, ask your child to reward, and then gently stroke the cat.

2 Using treats to tempt her, encourage your cat to climb onto your child's lap. Ask your child to remain quiet and relaxed. Once she is on your child's lap, ask your child to briefly stroke her, then praise and reward. Do not force the cat to stay – allow her to escape if she tries.

3 Repeat these exercises over several days, gradually increasing the duration. Encourage your child to be calm and positive and never to squeeze, shout at, or restrain the cat. Remember, for this to work, your cat must dictate the pace; never maintain a level of intensity that she resists.

Massage

Cat massage has stress-relieving properties and is a good opportunity to give your cat a thorough body check. Using your thumbs, gently rub your cat, starting at her head and using slow circular motions. Work down her neck, back, and legs. You may have to reduce the massage time for older or nervous cats.

Handling older cats

Older cats might not enjoy being handled; they may suffer from chronic pain, have had little socialization, or be easily scared. Therefore it is important to bear the following in mind:

● Frequently, older cats have a lower threshold to being touched. It is important to respect them and their tolerance levels.
● When working through the exercises above, stop if you see any signs of anxiety.
● Be patient and be prepared to go over the exercises more often than you might have to with a younger cat.
● Never force, restrain, or shout at your cat.

Day 8

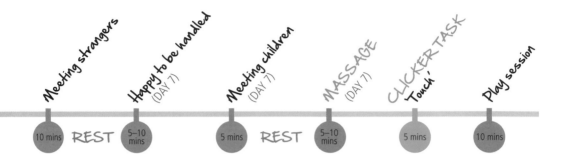

Meeting strangers	Happy to be handled (DAY 7)	Meeting children (DAY 7)	MASSAGE (DAY 7)	CLICKER TASK 'Touch'	Play session
10 mins REST 5–10 mins		5 mins REST 5–10 mins		5 mins	10 mins

Meeting strangers

It is important to familiarize your cat with visitors to your home. Relaxed cats will need only basic training (skip to steps 4–6). However, under-socialized and timid cats will require more reassurance and training.

1 Place your cat in her sanctuary room, plug in a pheromone diffuser, and leave the door slightly ajar. Arrange for a friend to ring the doorbell and invite them into the living room. Avoid any interaction with your cat, should she happen to appear.

2 Have a brief chat with your visitor and then visit your cat in her sanctuary room. Speak to her softly and then take an interactive toy and casually move it around. If she engages in play, praise and reward her. If she is in hiding, leave her for now.

3 After about 15 minutes, go back to your visitor then repeat step 2. Hopefully your cat will follow you from her sanctuary room this time, but it may take several sessions to build her confidence. Remember to stay calm and reward any positive steps.

Clicker tips

- Keep the sessions short, positive, and fun.
- Be consistent.
- Click/treat immediately when you elicit the desired behaviour.
- Only click once to mark the behaviour.
- Do not click unwanted behaviour.
- Always end the session on a positive note.
- Be patient and never punish your cat.

Clicker task

'Touch'

When your cat has mastered touching the target stick, introduce the cue word – 'touch'.

1 Take the target, and say the cue word 'touch' as soon as her nose makes contact with the target – click and treat immediately.

2 To reinforce this behaviour, use short training sessions throughout the day. Be sure to consistently click and treat every successful attempt and always link the cue word with the behaviour.

4 When your cat decides to enter the room, greet her in a soft voice, but continue talking to your visitor. Ask your guest to avoid eye contact and interaction. Everything must be done at your cat's pace. Reward calm behaviour and any positive advances she makes towards your guest.

5 If she is reserved and observing from a distance, try enticing her into the room with a toy. This should help to normalize things for her. If she does engage in play, give her a tasty reward and stroke her. Never force your cat to enter the room; she must always be the one to make the decision.

6 If she tries to interact with your visitor, ask them to reward her by tossing a treat to her. Then, get your guest to slowly extend his or her hand to the cat; if she wants to interact further, she will walk closer. Reward all positive behaviour. Repeat this exercise over a period of several days.

Day 9

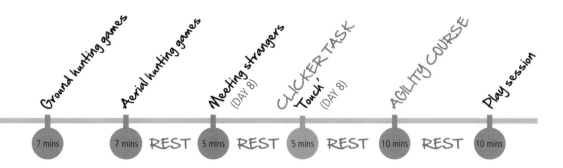

Ground hunting games — 7 mins

Aerial hunting games — 7 mins

REST

Meeting strangers (DAY 8) — 5 mins

REST

CLICKER TASK 'Touch' (DAY 8) — 5 mins

REST

AGILITY COURSE — 10 mins

REST

Play session — 10 mins

Ground hunting games

Play is an essential activity for cats of all ages. It is fun, mentally stimulating, a great way to prevent boredom and reduce anxiety, and it's a great form of exercise. And on top of all this, it provides a good opportunity for bonding with your cat.

1 Try attaching a toy mouse on a string to a wand-type toy. Hide the 'mouse' behind a piece of furniture, such as a table leg, then move the toy in a way that will stimulate your cat's prey drive. She will think that she's hunting a real mouse!

2 Start by subtly quivering the toy to get your cat's attention. Remember, in the wild a rodent would not be running directly in front of a cat. Move the toy mouse slowly away from your cat, and then hold it in position for a few seconds.

3 Move the toy like prey by alternating between fast and slow motions. Continue to do this until your cat stalks, follows, and eventually pounces on the toy. Allow your cat to have several captures of the toy so she does not get frustrated.

Aerial hunting games

Cats have incredible stamina and play gives them an outlet for this energy, while giving them an opportunity to satisfy their innate hunting drive. This exercise will allow your cat to really jump and stretch.

1 Use the toy from your ground hunting game (opposite), but attach a feather to it as well. Move the toy in a way that simulates a bird in flight. This will appeal to cats that have a head for heights and prefer more aerial pursuits.

2 Move the toy quickly up and away from the cat. If your cat 'captures' the toy, allow her to experience the thrill of success. This will serve to build her confidence.

3 To end the game, slowly wind down the movements of the toy, as if the 'prey' is getting tired. When the prey gets slower, allow your cat one last grand capture and end the play session by giving your cat a tasty treat.

Avoid bubbles and lasers

Using laser pens and bubbles as toys might seem like fun to you, but for your cat it is very frustrating as she never actually 'captures' anything. Ultimately this can lead to compulsive behaviour. Interactive toys, such as the ones shown here, are far better at stimulating your cat and providing her with the reward she deserves.

Agility course

Create a cat agility course using cardboard boxes, chairs or tables. Then encourage your cat to jump from one to another, using play as an enticement.

You will be surprised at how stimulating this will be for your cat and what a wonderful bonding experience playing with your cat can be.

Day 10

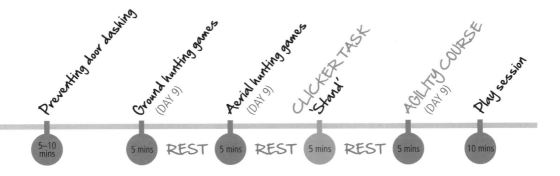

Preventing door dashing

Ground hunting games (DAY 9)

Aerial hunting games (DAY 9)

CLICKER TASK 'Stand'

AGILITY COURSE (DAY 9)

Play session

5–10 mins | 5 mins | REST | 5 mins | REST | 5 mins | REST | 5 mins | 10 mins

Preventing door dashing

If your cat makes a dash for it whenever you open the front door, she is at risk of being involved in an accident, or even disappearing forever. Follow these training exercises to prevent this. Younger cats should practise for 10 minutes; older ones for five only.

1 Establish a 'greeting zone' in your house. This is where you will encourage your cat to stay when you leave and arrive at the house. A place by the window is ideal. To help your cat associate this area with good things, leave treats, and groom and play with her there.

2 To train your cat to 'stay' in this area while you exit the house, call her to her designated spot and reward her as soon as she gets there. Once settled, hold your hand out, palm facing towards her and give the cue word 'stay'. Reward her immediately.

3 Gradually extend the duration of the 'stay'. When she's settled, give the cue word 'stay', but this time wait a couple of seconds before rewarding her. If she breaks the stay and moves or jumps down, start the exercise again. Be calm and patient!

21-Day Training Plan

Training tips

- Do not expect too much, too soon.
- Keep the sessions short and finish on a positive note.
- Train when your cat is hungry, using tasty treats.
- Be consistent, calm and patient.
- Even the best-trained cats can have lapses, so be vigilant.
- Ensure your cat is microchipped, just in case she leaves the house and gets lost.
- Remember that by providing an enriching and stimulating environment, you will reduce your cat's desire to rush out of the door.

Clicker task

'Stand'

Start with your cat in the sit position. Scratch her just above the base of her tail – she should automatically lift her bottom and stand up. The moment she stands up, click and treat. Repeat this several times to reinforce the behaviour. Once she has mastered this, try adding the cue word 'stand' as soon as she rises.

4 When she consistently stays for a count of five seconds, start adding a few distractions. Ask her to stay and then take a couple of steps backwards; reward her when she stays in position. Gradually increase the distance and repeat over several days.

5 Before leaving for work, call your cat to the greeting zone. Ask her to 'stay', then praise and reward. Leave a few treats and a toy with her and calmly walk for the door. If she jumps down, place her back in position and repeat the exercise.

6 On returning from work, only give her attention once she is in the greeting zone. Always praise and reward this. Whenever you enter or leave the house, do not engage with her until she is where she should be. Make sure that you are always consistent.

Day 11

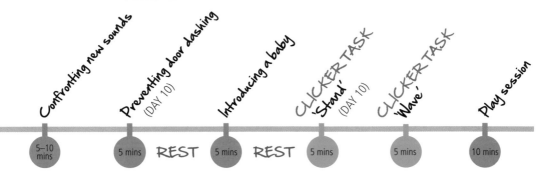

Confronting new sounds

Preventing door dashing
(DAY 10)

Introducing a baby

CLICKER TASK
'Stand'
(DAY 10)

CLICKER TASK
'Wave'

Play session

5–10 mins   5 mins   REST   5 mins   REST   5 mins   5 mins   10 mins

Confronting new sounds

Kittenhood is the perfect time to familiarize your cat with unusual sounds, although you can use these exercises to desensitize older cats too (but practise for 5 minutes only).

1 Vacuum cleaners are scary and unpredictable to cats. To desensitize her to their loud noise (and to other noisy objects), ask a friend to switch on the vacuum cleaner in a different room to your cat. Meanwhile, praise and reward her with treats or a play session. Keep the exercise short and stop if she becomes stressed.

2 Now, bring the vacuum into the same room as your cat, ask your friend to switch it on and very gradually bring it closer, while you continue to reward and praise your cat, speaking in a calm, soft voice. Monitor for signs of stress throughout and be prepared to move the vacuum further away if she appears anxious.

3 If your cat appears untroubled by the noise of the vacuum, continue to move it closer to her, making sure that she is at a distance where she feels comfortable. Continue to reward her with her favourite treats. If she looks anxious, stop and try again later.

Introducing a baby

The sound and presence of a baby can be overwhelming to a cat. However, there are several steps you can take to improve an introduction and create a lasting friendship.

Before the baby arrives

When the baby arrives

Before the baby's arrival, create a sanctuary for your cat with all of her resources, including a pheromone diffuser. Familiarize her to the sound of a baby crying by using a pre-recording on low volume and reward her for relaxed behaviour. Finally, try wearing baby lotion and talcum powder to familiarize your cat to new-baby smells.

When the baby arrives, keep your cat's routine as normal as possible and give her the same attention as before. In a quiet room, allow her to observe, approach, and sniff the baby, but be sure to supervise all interactions and reward all positive behaviour. Never force her to get close to the baby and make sure she can always retreat to her sanctuary.

Dealing with fireworks

- Create a 'sanctuary room' for your cat and plug in a pheromone diffuser.
- Ensure she has hiding places, such as cardboard boxes, to make her feel safer.
- Close all windows, doors, and cat flap to prevent her from leaving the house.
- Provide calming music to mask the noise of the fireworks.
- Stay calm and act normally – your cat will only pick up on your anxieties otherwise.

Clicker task

'Wave'
With your cat sitting on a table, move a tasty treat back and forth in front of her at about face level. When she attempts to reach for the treat, click and reward her. Repeat the exercise. Be patient, as this skill takes time to learn.

Day 12

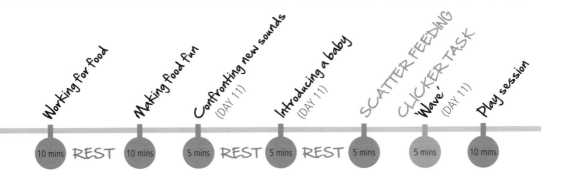

Working for food — 10 mins | REST | Making food fun — 10 mins | Confronting new sounds (DAY 11) — 5 mins | REST | Introducing a baby (DAY 11) — 5 mins | REST | SCATTER FEEDING — 5 mins | CLICKER TASK 'Wave' (DAY 11) — 5 mins | Play session — 10 mins

Working for food

Cats are natural hunters and in their natural environment they spend hours every day hunting for food. However, living in a household means they do not need to hunt for food and this can lead to under-stimulation, reduced activity, and boredom. Encouraging a cat to work for her food is an effective way to enrich her life.

1 Divide a portion of your cat's regular food into several small bowls. Place these in highly visible, easy-to-reach areas around your house. To get her meal, she will have to look throughout the house for it. This encourages natural foraging and predatory-type behaviours.

2 When she is consistently finding the small bowls, try placing the food in more difficult-to-reach areas. The idea is to gradually make the task more difficult. For example, try a cupboard top or behind a curtain. Her search for her food will stimulate her, both mentally and physically.

3 Once mastered, it's time to make the task more challenging again! Hide small portions of food in very obscure places. You can also try covering the portion with a cloth or cardboard. This will make mealtimes much more interesting and keep her active.

Making food fun

Cats love to play with their food, which isn't so much fun for their prey! You can make a few simple gadgets that will enable your cat to fulfil her natural inclinations and work for her food.

1 Wash and dry a plastic water bottle and make a few holes on the outside, large enough so that dry food kibble can fall out. Then put some of your cat's food allowance into the bottle. She should soon figure out what to do.

2 Stick together six empty toilet rolls to form a pyramid. Place a portion of your cat's food allowance in several of the rolls. Make it easy at first by placing the food at the front then increase the difficulty by pushing the food further in.

3 Make a puzzle-box feeder by sealing a cardboard box and cutting a few holes on each side. Ensure the holes are big enough for your cat to fit her paw in, but not her head. Show your cat the box and let her see you place some food inside.

Scatter feeding

Take a small portion of your cat's dry food allowance then throw a kibble on the floor away from your cat. She will pursue it as she would prey.

Vary your throws to make it more difficult – throw a kibble in the air or throw faster and further. Watch how quickly her hunting skills develop.

The benefits of activity feeding

The exercises shown above and opposite are some of the ways that you can involve your cat in 'activity feeding'. This provides your cat with the following benefits:

- Encourages mental stimulation.
- Prevents boredom.
- Provides additional exercise.
- Provides stimulation associated with prey capture.
- Reduces boredom-related destructive behaviours.
- Prevents cats from gulping their meal too quickly.

Don't be tempted to give your cat extra food – the food provided for the activity feeding exercises must come from her daily allowance.

Day 13

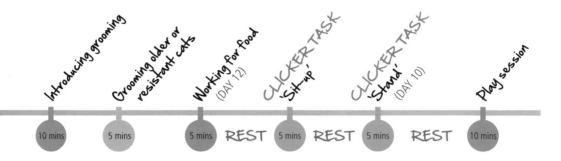

Introducing grooming — 10 mins

Grooming older or resistant cats — 5 mins

Working for food (DAY 12) — 5 mins

REST

CLICKER TASK 'Sit-up' — 5 mins

REST

CLICKER TASK 'Stand' (DAY 10) — 5 mins

REST

Play session — 10 mins

Introducing grooming

All cats require regular grooming to maintain their coat and also strengthen bonding. It's best to familiarize your cat with grooming from an early age but if you have an older cat, try the exercise opposite first.

1 It is important that your cat views grooming as a positive experience. Begin by placing the brush near your cat and reward her for any advances she makes towards it. Then try holding the brush in your hand and praise her when she comes to investigate. You can groom on a table, but watch your cat vigilantly for safety reasons.

2 Next, alternate between one gentle hand stroke and one brush stroke. Restrict the brushing to easier regions, such as her head, chin, and back, speaking to her in a soft voice and rewarding her as you do so. Repeat this several times.

3 Try the stroke/brush exercise on more difficult areas such as her back legs. Start off with one brush stroke, gradually increasing as you go. Be patient, proceed very slowly, and always reward your cat for any positive response. Stop if you get a negative reaction, trying again later once she's calm.

Grooming older or resistant cats

For older cats, or cats with an aversion to grooming, the training process will take longer and you will need to build her trust first by gently stroking and rewarding her with no brush in sight.

1 Instead of using a brush, try a grooming glove, which is softer and will familiarize her to something other than your hand. Progress very slowly, keeping the gentle strokes to her head, neck, and back. Always praise and reward.

2 When she tolerates the grooming glove, try steps 1 to 3 (opposite page). Initially, restrict the grooming to her head and neck; only progress if she remains relaxed. If she becomes anxious, you are progressing too quickly and need to go back a few steps. Always finish on a positive note.

Grooming tips

How often should I groom my cat?
Aim for several grooming sessions per week. During spring and autumn, when cats shed their fur, sessions may need to be more frequent. Begin with a soft-bristled brush, before moving on to other grooming equipment.

Grooming long-haired cats
Long-haired cats require extra maintenance: groom daily, and check the fur under the base of the tail and the back of the hind-legs to ensure it's not soiled. Try to tease any matted fur out with your fingers. If you are unable to do so, consult your vet or a professional cat groomer.

Above all, keep sessions short, and stay calm and patient.

Clicker task

'Sit-up'
When your cat is sitting, hold a treat just above her nose. Click and reward when one or both paws lift slightly off the ground. Repeat several times, moving the treat over her head and only click when her paws lift higher off the ground. Gradually hold the treat higher and eventually your cat will execute a complete 'sit-up'.

Day 14

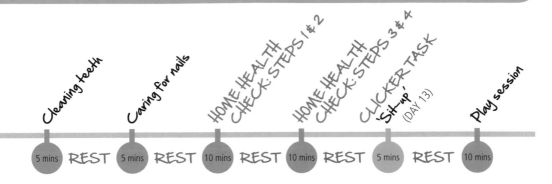

Cleaning teeth · Caring for nails · HOME HEALTH CHECK: STEPS 1 & 2 · HOME HEALTH CHECK: STEPS 3 & 4 · CLICKER TASK 'Sit-up' (DAY 13) · Play session

5 mins · REST · 5 mins · REST · 10 mins · REST · 10 mins · REST · 5 mins · REST · 10 mins

Cleaning teeth

Keeping your cat's teeth clean is an essential part of the grooming process. Good dental hygiene is crucial for good health and helps to avoid gum disease and tartar build-up.

1 With your cat on your lap, gently stroke her head and then the sides of her mouth. Reward her immediately. If she tolerates this, try touching her lips, and then if she allows it, touch her teeth. It's important to reward her during each stage.

2 Next, place a piece of gauze around your finger and dip it into water from drained canned tuna, then gently rub your cat's teeth with the gauze. Keep the session short and reward immediately on completion. Repeat often so she becomes comfortable with the procedure.

3 Using a cat toothbrush and paste, gently brush a couple of her teeth. End the session with praise and reward. Later in the day try brushing a few more teeth, gradually building up her tolerance.

Caring for nails

Keeping your cat's claws trimmed is an important part of maintaining your pet's health, keeping them free from dirt and infections. It also protects her and you from unwanted scratching.

1 The first step in nail maintenance is for your cat to allow you to touch her paws. Take her paw between your thumb and finger and gently apply a little pressure. Release the pressure and reward. Then, gently press on her paw to extend her claws and reward again.

2 Next, allow her to investigate the clippers by placing them nearby. To get her used to the sound of the clippers take a strand of uncooked spaghetti and cut a few pieces off the strand while simultaneously rewarding her.

3 Gradually build up your cat's tolerance by pretending to clip her claws. If she accepts this, clip just the tip of one claw (avoiding the quick) and then reward her. Be prepared to clip just one or two claws at a time and end on a positive note. Repeat the exercise over several days.

Home health check

1 Start with your cat's eyes, which should be bright and free of discharge. Next, look at her ears, which should be clean, pink, and odour-free. Ear-scratching or head shaking may be a sign of ear mites.

2 Check her mouth during teeth cleaning; her gums should be pink and her mouth free of foul odour. Her nose should be free of excessive discharge and will normally feel dry.

3 Rub your hands down her body, checking for lumps and bumps. Examine her coat for tiny black specks that could be a sign of fleas.

4 Finally, check her anal area for redness, discharge, or any visible worms; tapeworms resemble small bits of rice. If you find any abnormalities during the health check, consult your vet. Reward your cat throughout.

Day 15

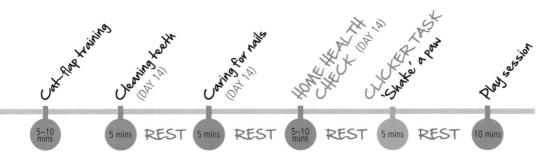

Cat-flap training | Cleaning teeth (DAY 14) | Caring for nails (DAY 14) | HOME HEALTH CHECK (DAY 14) | CLICKER TASK 'Shake' a paw | Play session

5–10 mins | 5 mins | REST | 5 mins | REST | 5–10 mins | REST | 5 mins | REST | 10 mins

Cat-flap training

Many cats teach themselves to use a cat flap though trial and error. However, for kittens and timid cats, a cat flap can be a frightening experience and it is important to train them to learn that there is nothing to fear. Restrict training to 5 minutes for older cats.

1 Your cat must learn that the flap is an entrance and exit to the home. Start by leaving the cat flap fully open by securing with a piece of tape or string. The key is to praise and reward any advances towards the opening.

2 It is less frightening for your cat if you entice her to *enter* her place of safety, rather than leave it. Ask a friend to hold her outside the door, then tempt her through the flap from the inside with food or a piece of string. If she steps through, reward and praise.

3 Once step 2 is mastered, try encouraging her to *exit* using a similar method from outside the flap. Repeat this exercise several times. Do not rush, nor push her through the flap. This should be done at your cat's pace.

Clicker task

'Shake' a paw

1 With your cat sitting, extend your right hand and gently touch her right paw. If she lifts her paw (even slightly), click and treat. If she doesn't move, then gently lift her paw, click then treat. Repeat this exercise several times.

2 Practise step 1 until she has mastered it, then add a cue word. Move your right hand towards her, giving the cue 'shake'. If she lifts her paw as before, click then reward. If she moves her paw only a little, still click and treat. Keep practising!

How to signal 'no exit allowed'

Ideally, keep your cat indoors between dusk and dawn. Overnight, many cats are outside and competition for resources is high.

Locking your cat flap may confuse your cat and she may try to push her way out regardless. Instead, place a barrier across the cat flap, such as a board or towel. She will learn to associate this signal with being unable to exit.

Use this technique as soon as you start cat-flap training.

4 Gradually lower the flap over several days. Although she will still be able to fit through the gap, she will have to learn to push it with her head or paws in order to pass through. Encourage her with food and play, rewarding all successful attempts.

5 Lower the flap a little bit more, so it becomes more of an obstruction and she has to push with a little force. If she struggles with this stage, go back a few steps; some cats learn the technique more quickly than others.

6 Finally, practise with the flap completely closed. Initially, you might have to show her lots of encouragement, but she should soon learn that going through the flap is easy and not scary or painful.

Day 16

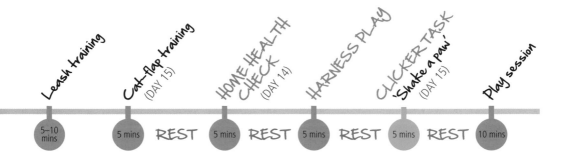

Leash training	Cat-flap training (DAY 15)		HOME HEALTH CHECK (DAY 14)		HARNESS PLAY		CLICKER TASK 'Shake a paw' (DAY 15)		Play session
5–10 mins	5 mins	REST	5 mins	REST	5 mins	REST	5 mins	REST	10 mins

Leash training

Some cats can be successfully trained to walk on a leash. This allows owners and their cats, particularly indoor cats, to have a safe, supervised, and fun time outdoors. Remember, some older cats or nervous cats may need shorter sessions.

1 Place the harness on the floor and allow your cat to sniff and investigate it. If possible, try to collect some of her facial pheromones with a cloth. Rub this onto the harness, which will then smell familiar to her.

2 When she seems relaxed, gently place the harness on your cat, keeping it loose, and distract her with some of her favourite treats. Carefully take the harness back off, and repeat this step several times. Each time you put the harness on and she remains calm, reward her.

3 When your cat is relaxed and happy with step 2, fasten the harness, distracting her with her favourite treats if necessary. The key is to keep everything positive!

21-Day Training Plan

Harness play

Once you have been through the leash training (opposite and below) with your cat and she is comfortable with the harness, have a five-minute play session with the harness attached. Try either a ground or aerial hunting game (see pages 42–43).

Leash-training tips

- Cat-walking jackets are similar to harnesses, but are safer for the cat, and more easily accepted.
- Make sure to get the correct fit and adjust it properly for comfort and safety.
- Proceed slowly. Your cat's comfort level is paramount, and leash training can take weeks rather than days.
- If venturing into the garden, make sure her vaccinations and flea treatments are up-to-date.
- Once your cat has had a taste of the outdoors, be careful that she doesn't bolt for the door unrestrained.

4 Let her walk around wearing the harness with no leash attached. Repeat this stage several times, gradually increasing the duration. Once your cat is accepting of the harness, attach the leash for short periods. Let her wander around indoors with it trailing. Reward her, then take hold of the leash, call her to you and reward her when she comes. Repeat this often before venturing into the garden.

5 Allow your cat to step outside of her own free will – don't tug her. Encourage her by calling her name in a soft tone and reward each time she responds. Don't venture far on the first few occasions; just outside the back door will be enough to begin with.

6 Over several days, gradually increase the distance until she is happily walking in the garden. Keep rewarding her for positive actions. If she shows any signs of stress then go back a few steps – remember, this should all be at her pace.

Day 17

Cat carrier training | 5–10 mins | REST | Leash training (DAY 16) | 5 mins | REST | HARNESS PLAY (DAY 16) | 5 mins | REST | CLICKER TASK 'High five!' | 5 mins | CLICKER TASK 'Sit-up' (DAY 13) | 5 mins | Play session | 10 mins

Cat carrier training

A cat carrier is essential for taking your cat to a cattery or to the vet. You can teach your cat to enter the carrier, but if she is fearful, note that training can take weeks. Limit sessions to 5 minutes for older cats.

1 Place the carrier in a room that is very familiar to your cat. Put a cosy blanket inside the carrier and remove the door or lid. If she investigates, reward her immediately. If she ignores it, do not force her into the carrier.

2 Place a few treats near to the carrier to entice her to come closer. If she seems nervous and refuses to eat the treats, you have probably put them too close. Move them back and give her time.

3 When she confidently takes treats from near the carrier, it's time to move on. Place a treat inside the carrier. If she willingly approaches and takes the treat, try gradually moving the treats further inside.

4 Replace the door (or lid) and leave it open. Place a treat inside the carrier; when she enters, close the door for a couple of seconds, re-open and reward. Repeat this process several times, increasing the time that the door is closed.

Add the verbal cue: say 'enter'. Each time you place a treat into the carrier, say 'enter'; use a happy tone and reward any positive steps. Be prepared to take a few steps back if she seems anxious or unsure.

5 Finally, when your cat is inside the carrier, close the door and gently lift the carrier off the floor for a few seconds only. Reward her when you re-open the door. Extend the time the door is closed and increase the height you lift the carrier off the floor.

Carrier tips

- The carrier should always be put in a safe place when your cat is inside, providing your cat with a sense of security.
- There should be enough space for her to stand without crouching, so she is able to turn around.
- Don't bring the carrier out for trips to the vet or cattery only; she will quickly form negative associations.
- Following any unpleasant trips in the carrier, perform the training steps again.
- Always check the door is properly closed and the latches are fastened when your cat is inside.

Clicker task

'High five!'

1 Hold your hand above your cat's paw. When her paw makes contact, click, treat, and give her lots of praise. If she fails to touch your hand, withhold the reward and lower your hand slightly before trying again.

2 Raise your hand to a 'high five' position. If she connects, click and reward, if she doesn't, lower your hand. When she is reliably connecting, add the cue 'High five!'.

Day 18

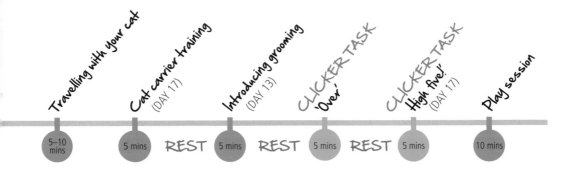

Travelling with your cat
Cat carrier training (DAY 17)
Introducing grooming (DAY 13)
CLICKER TASK 'Over'
CLICKER TASK 'High five!' (DAY 17)
Play session

5–10 mins | 5 mins | REST | 5 mins | REST | 5 mins | REST | 5 mins | 10 mins

Travelling with your cat

It is important to desensitize your cat to any fear of travelling in the car, making the trips to the vet, for instance, less stressful for both of you. Restrict sessions to 5 minutes for older cats.

1 Encourage your cat into her carrier and carefully place it onto the back seat of the car. Leave the car door open, sit next to her and reward calm behaviour. After a minute take her back into the house, reward and praise; repeat several times.

2 For the next stage, repeat step 1, but this time close the car door. Stay in the car with her for a minute or two and then take her back into the house. Reward her with a treat or play session.

3 Next, start the engine. Leave the engine running for a minute, then switch off and take her back into the house. If she shows any signs of anxiety go back a stage or two. Take things slowly, keeping to your cat's pace.

Clicker task

'Over'

1 Set up a small jump by using a pole or a piece of board. Ask a friend to hold your cat on one side of the jump with you on the other. Using the target stick, lure her over the jump. Be patient as the first jump is the most difficult. Click and reward on completion.

2 When she is reliably jumping across, add the verbal cue 'over', then click and reward once she's landed on the other side. Gradually, you can increase the height of the jump, or use different obstacles.

4 Next, take a short trip down the driveway, and then return immediately. Take her back into the house, praise and reward. Take this part of the training very slowly as the motion of the car may scare her; be sure to always drive smoothly and speak to her in a soft, calming voice.

5 If your cat seems relaxed then gradually extend the length of time that she spends in the car, and try to have several training sessions over the next few days.

To help your cat associate the car with positive activities rather than negative ones, ask your vet if you can drop by for a social visit only. She will learn that sometimes she gets petted and fussed at the vet, rather than just prodded and poked!

Travel tips

- If your cat shows an aversion to travel from the outset, make sure you proceed very slowly.
- Try spraying the carrier and the inside of the car with a pheromone preparation 30 minutes before any training.
- If your cat shows an aversion to engine sounds, play a 'sounds' CD in the house at progressively higher volumes to get her used to the noise of the car.
- Play some calm and relaxing music in the car while you are driving to help put your cat at ease.
- Make sure you secure the carrier on the back seat using the seat belt.

Day 19

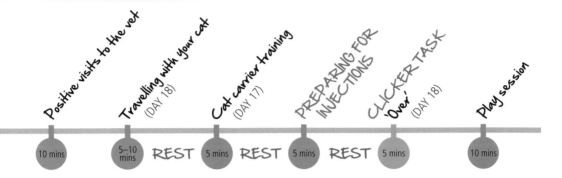

Positive visits to the vet

Traveling with your cat (DAY 18)

Cat carrier training (DAY 17)

PREPARING FOR INJECTIONS

CLICKER TASK 'Over' (DAY 18)

Play session

10 mins | 5–10 mins | REST | 5 mins | REST | 5 mins | REST | 5 mins | 10 mins

Positive visits to the vet

Kittens can be taught to form positive associations with trips to the vet. With time and patience it is also possible to minimize the stress for a cat that has already begun to fear visits to the vet.

1 On arrival at the surgery, give the receptionist your cat's favourite treat to offer your cat. Praise your cat, speaking in a calm and reassuring voice. Keep the carrier elevated on a chair or on your lap, and cover the carrier if she appears nervous.

2 In the examination room, unclip and remove the lid from the carrier. Your cat still has the security of remaining in the bottom half. Try distracting her with a tasty treat. If the vet requires her on the examination table, place her blanket down first to provide a sense of security.

3 Remain calm and handle your cat gently. She will respond better to this than to restraint. If your cat is scheduled for a vaccination, distract her with a tasty treat and keep everything positive. If possible make frequent trips to the vet for social visits and then return home.

4 If you have another cat, she will notice that the returning cat has brought home unfamiliar scents (of the clinic and other animals). The returning cat looks the same, but her scent cannot be recognized by her friend at home, and this often results in fighting.

5 To prevent fights when you arrive home, take her to a spare room without any contact with the other cat. Take a soft cloth and gently rub the stay-at-home cat to gather her scent. Next rub this scent onto the cat in the spare room.

6 Leave her in the room for about an hour. Both cats should now smell the same, and they will recognize each other as friends. Bring them back together with the help of a few treats and a play session. Keep everything positive.

Preparing for injections

1 Stroke your cat on her head and then continue down to the back of her neck. Praise and reward. Slowly move your hand towards the back of her neck and apply a little pressure for a couple of seconds, click then treat; repeat several times.

2 Gradually increase the duration of the exercise and the intensity of the pressure. If she is relaxed, gently try lifting a bit of skin at the back of her neck; praise and reward immediately.

3 If she tolerates this, lift a bit of her skin and gently touch with the blunt end of a pen, praise, and reward. Repeat over several days, always ending on a positive note. She will soon learn that remaining calm while being handled results in something positive.

Day 20

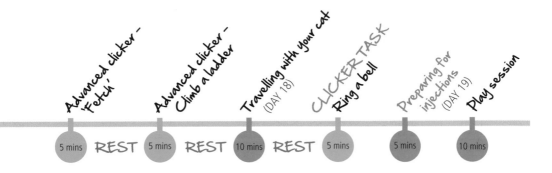

Advanced clicker - 'Fetch'

Advanced clicker - Climb a ladder

Travelling with your cat (DAY 18)

CLICKER TASK Ring a bell

Preparing for injections (DAY 19)

Play session

5 mins | REST | 5 mins | REST | 10 mins | REST | 5 mins | 5 mins | 10 mins

Advanced clicker – 'Fetch'

If you've been following the clicker training tasks so far, you will be ready to attempt more advanced exercises. Clicker training is stimulating for your cat, will help prevent behaviour problems, and above all else, it is fun!

1 Training a cat to retrieve a toy exercises her natural hunting skills. Certain breeds will excel, others will take time and patience. Apply some 'tuna water' to your cat's favourite toy to make it more attractive, then throw it past her, out of her reach.

2 Reward any positive move she makes; if she walks over to the toy, sniffs or picks it up, click and treat. Repeat this exercise several times. If she picks the toy up, wait a second then click and treat. Be patient, it can take many sessions to get her to pick the toy up.

3 If she brings the toy towards you, click then reward. She will release the toy to eat her reward, so take it in readiness to throw again. If she is reliably retrieving the toy, add the cue word 'fetch' as you throw it. Take things slowly and always end on a positive note.

Clicker task

Ring a bell

1 Training your cat to ring a bell is a very cute trick, but BEWARE...this can result in her training you to respond to her bell ring! Secure small bells to a piece of string or ribbon and suspend them from the back of a chair. Call your cat over.

2 Hold a treat behind the bells to encourage your cat to reach for it with her paw. If she touches the bells, then click and treat. If you have taught her to 'wave' previously, you could give this cue and see if she accidentally touches the bells.

3 When your cat touches the bells eight times out of ten, introduce the cue word 'ring'. Click then treat the moment she makes contact with the bells. Repeat this exercise daily.

Advanced clicker – Climb a ladder

This is a great trick that is quite simple to teach, especially if your cat is attuned to a target stick. Follow the exercises below and impress your friends with your clever climbing cat!

1 Call your cat over to a small stepladder and encourage her to follow the target stick up the first few rungs. When she reaches the top platform, click and reward. Cats learn at different speeds, so be patient.

2 Next, with the aid of the target stick, slowly lure her back down the rungs. When she reaches the bottom, click, reward, and praise her.

3 Practise this exercise over several days, and remember to keep the training positive. When she is comfortable going up and down the ladder, add the cue words 'climb', and when she achieves successive steps, be sure to click and reward her.

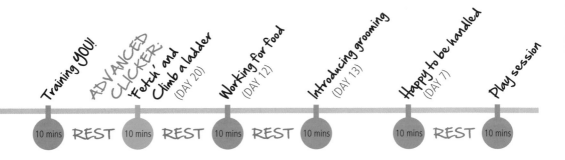

Day 21

Training YOU!

ADVANCED CLICKER: Fetch' and Climb a ladder (DAY 20)

Working for food (DAY 12)

Introducing grooming (DAY 13)

Happy to be handled (DAY 7)

Play session

10 mins   REST   10 mins   REST   10 mins   REST   10 mins   10 mins   REST   10 mins

Training YOU!

This last day of the programme is dedicated to *you*, the owner. Having come this far, it is important for your cat to continue to grow into a well-adjusted, well-behaved, problem-free individual. To achieve this, it is essential that you integrate many of the training exercises covered over the past three weeks into your cat's daily routine.

Many behavioural problems stem from cats not being able to engage in their natural behaviours, and owners putting unrealistic expectations onto them. If you are at work all day, you must provide plenty of activities and stimulation in your absence. This 21-day programme is a starting point to ensure that your cat's needs are catered for on a daily basis.

The exercises will have undoubtedly challenged, stimulated, and occupied her (and you), reducing the likelihood of inappropriate behaviours occurring. At the same time they will have strengthened the bond between you and your cat.

The 'Essential daily tasks' opposite should be integrated into your cat's routine on a daily basis. It won't take much time out of your day, but it will make a huge difference to your cat.

Essential daily tasks

The tasks below constitute those that are strongly recommended to be carried out on a daily basis in order to achieve an all-round happy, healthy, and well-behaved cat.

Interactive play

As a minimum requirement, have 15 minutes of interactive play in both the morning and evening, before feeding. Make the sessions fun and stimulating. End the sessions with a reward and praise.

Activity feeding

Cats are natural-born hunters and by providing activity feeding, your cat's life will be enriched. Integrate the exercises on pages 48–49 into her daily routine morning and evening.

Grooming and health check

Get into the habit of giving your cat a daily groom. Conduct the session when she is relaxed, preferably after eating (see pages 50–51). It is also an ideal opportunity to give her a quick health check (see page 53).

Handling

It is important that you continue to handle your cat on a daily basis (see pages 38–39). Not only will this further increase your bond with one another, but it will also make it easier to groom, transport, and medicate your cat.

Clicker training

Not only is clicker training a great source of mental stimulation for your cat, it also allows you to teach her tricks that are an extension of her natural behaviour, such as climbing. Conduct one or two short sessions daily.

Maintain consistency and routine, and have fun!

Remember, cats are happiest when their lives have routine. Make sure that her life is full of consistency, and above all else, plenty of fun!

Part 3:

50 Quick Fixes

Fast and easy ways to solve tricky problems

1: Eating indoor plants

Most cats like chewing on grass, probably because it is a quickly digestible source of vitamins, minerals, and roughage. Indoor cats may start to nibble on houseplants if they do not have access to grass. However, this can be very dangerous as some houseplants are toxic and can lead to illness, and sometimes death. There are two ways to deal with this behaviour:

● Keep only houseplants that are safe for cats and use a deterrent, such as a 'plant-safe' anti-chew spray. This should taste repulsive to your cat and deter future nibbling of sprayed plants.
● Provide your cat with an acceptable alternative such as seedling grass sprouts, available from pet stores. The grass can be planted in containers so your cat can access it easily.

2: Raiding the bin

Even if a cat is well-fed, there are always those that will actively raid the kitchen bin in search of scraps. There may be an underlying medical reason for this, so it might be worth consulting your vet if your cat does this. If your cat is given a clean bill of health, you could try the following tips:

● Try relocating your bin to a cupboard so your cat cannot gain access. Failing that, fit a child-proof latch to keep it securely closed.
● Place some double-sided sticky tape around the top of the bin; cats dislike getting their paws sticky.
● Provide several small meals a day at regular times, or use a timed automatic feeder. You could also try an activity feeder which should help keep her attention away from the bin!

50 Quick Fixes

3: Miaowing for food

Obesity is an ever-increasing problem in the cat world and demands for food are thought to be one of the main culprits. If your cat has got a clean bill of health and is fed a regular balanced diet, but still cries for food, then she has learned that miaowing often leads to a tasty snack! To avoid unnecessary feeding, try the following:

- Ignore any demands for food. Wait until she is quiet, then feed her.
- Have a 10-minute play session prior to feeding; this imitates a cat's natural behaviour in the wild – hunt then feast.
- Feed little and often.
- Introduce activity feeding (see pages 48–49).

4: Eating too fast

If your cat eats her food like it's her last supper, only to vomit it up a few minutes later, the following reasons might explain her behaviour:

- She may have had a tough start to life, not knowing when her next meal would be.
- She may be bored and lacking in stimulation.
- She may be stressed if eating too close to other pets.
- She may have a medical problem, such as parasites or hyperthyroidism.

The following tips can help your cat to slow down:

- Divide her food into several smaller meals.
- Try an automatic timed feeder, which will allow you to time and portion-control her food.
- Introduce puzzle feeders –these will slow down your cat's eating and provide her with stimulation (see page 49).
- If you have several cats, keep their food and water stations in separate areas of the house.

Quick fixes 1–4

5: Pulling food out of the bowl

Every so often a cat might pull her food out of the bowl on to the floor. There is, however, a rationale for this strange behaviour. Your cat is not being intentionally messy, she is just eating her meal in the easiest and quickest way possible. Some cats also dislike having their whiskers squashed into a bowl, especially flat-faced cats, such as Persians. To avoid a mess, try the following:

● Make sure your cat's bowl is shallow, as this might suit her better.
● Separate your cat's food and water stations.
● If she currently gets chunks of wet food, cut them up into smaller bite-sized pieces.
● Invest in a placemat with raised edges, as this will prevent any damage to your carpet or flooring.

6: Begging for food

Many cats get into the habit of begging for human food. Even if you only feed her from your plate occasionally, she will think that she has a right to your food. Furthermore, feeding a cat human food can upset her nutritional balance, pose health risks, and lead to obesity. If your cat has started begging for human food, try the following tips and your cat will soon learn that begging does not reap any rewards:

● Time her meals with your own mealtimes, and put her in a different room where you can close the doors. Keep her in this room until you have finished eating – then give her a reward.
● If you do allow your cat into the dining room while you are eating, ignore her begging behaviour completely.
● Try to remain calm; do not shout or push her away – this only leads to attention-seeking behaviour.
● Stimulate your cat by using a puzzle feeder for her food.

50 Quick Fixes

7: Refusing to drink

Fresh, clean water is essential for every cat, especially for those on a dry-food-only diet which has a low water content, of about 10 per cent. If your cat is refusing to drink from her bowl, consider the following:

- **Location** – make sure the water bowl is in a quiet place and set away from her food. Cats dislike food and water being close together.
- **Type of bowl** – consider different materials, particularly metal. Bacteria can quickly accumulate in plastic and ceramic bowls, and some cats do not like the smell of plastic.
- **Fresh is best** – change the water frequently; cats dislike stale water. Experiment with rainwater or bottled water as some cats prefer the taste to that of tap water.
- **Multi-cat households** – If you have a multi-cat household, provide multiple locations for water stations. This will reduce friction and conflict.
- **Try a water fountain** – some cats prefer these as an alternative.

8: Drinking from the toilet

As disgusting as it might sound to us, some cats like to drink from the toilet in preference to their water bowl, largely because the water is more appealing to them; it's fresher and may have more oxygen from recent flushings. The water in a cat's bowl may have been lying there for a while and become warm and stale. Cats like cold, fresh water.

The simplest way to solve this problem is by keeping the bathroom door closed and toilet lid down. Furthermore, ensure that your cat's regular water bowl is as appealing as possible by changing the water on a regular basis to make sure that it is clean and fresh.

9: Refusing to use the litter box

As frustrating as this unappealing habit might seem, your cat is not doing this on purpose or out of spite. The following tips can help solve the problem:

- Get your cat checked over by a vet to rule out any underlying medical issues.
- Do not punish her for toileting outside the box; this will only make the problem worse.
- Make sure your cat's litter box is clean.
- Avoid using litter-box liners.
- Ensure the litter box is an appropriate size for your cat.
- Remember that cats prefer unscented, fine-grain litter.
- Place the box in a private location away from her food.
- Multi-cat households must have one tray per cat, plus one extra.

10: Defecating outside the door

If your cat is deliberately depositing faeces in the open, away from her normal toileting area, and has made no attempt to cover it, it is known as 'middening'. This behaviour is a way of marking her territory in areas where she might feel particularly challenged and where new and unfamiliar scents are brought in from outside, such as doorways. To discourage this, consider doing the following:

- Try to remove any initial threats by covering cat flaps and blocking out nearby windows with an opaque window spray.
- Confine her to a small area for about a week (with resources) to help her feel more secure, then gradually reintroduce her to the rest of the house.
- Remove your shoes at the door to avoid bringing in challenging scents.

50 Quick Fixes

11: Elderly cats toileting outside the litter box

Sadly, appropriate elimination habits are often one of the first behaviours to deteriorate in elderly cats. It is important to separate behavioural issues from health issues, and therefore a visit to your vet to exclude medical problems is essential. The following simple steps can be taken to help your cat regain her dignity:

- If your cat has got mobility problems or reduced bladder control, provide extra litter boxes around the house in easy-to-locate areas.
- For cats with physical limitations, such as arthritis, provide litter boxes that have lower sides to minimize the need to climb.
- If your cat is no longer accurate when using her litter tray, try using a plastic storage box. Remove the lid of the box (if it has one) and cut an entrance in one end. This should prevent spills as the sides of storage boxes are much higher than regular litter trays.

12: Toileting in indoor plants

Unfortunately, potted houseplants can seem like the ideal location to toilet for both indoor and outdoor cats, who find the soft soil hard to resist. Here are some tips to help prevent this:

- Re-pot any affected plants using new potting soil; cats like to over-mark areas that they have already used.
- Transfer any faeces from the houseplant to a litter tray and place this tray near to where the problem is occurring.
- Make the houseplants as unappealing as possible to your cat by covering the soil with large irregular-shaped pebbles, prickly pinecones or broken shells.
- If all else fails, fit chicken wire over the soil to prevent your cat from digging, which is often a precursor to elimination.

13: Attacking toilet paper

Attacking and shredding toilet paper is a pastime that under-stimulated cats sometimes engage in to relieve boredom. To remedy this behaviour:

● Close the bathroom door before you leave for work.
● Provide your cat with a 10–15-minute intense interactive play session every morning and evening. This will provide her with stimulation and an outlet for her energy.
● Provide activity feeders and a range of stimulating toys.
● Install a toilet-roll holder that covers the top of the toilet roll, and prevents paws from being able to grab the end of the sheet.
● Place a small plastic cup half-filled with water on the top of the roll. When your cat tries to pull at the paper, she will get doused with water; this discourages even the most determined of cats!

14: Spraying on the curtains

Spraying outdoors is a completely normal behaviour for cats, male or female, neutered or not. Usually cats have no need to spray indoors because their home is perceived as safe and secure. However, if your cat starts to feel insecure or threatened in some way, she may start to spray indoors to boost her confidence. Spraying on curtains is usually indicative of an outside threat, such as a neighbouring cat. Try the following:

● Temporarily restrict her access to the outside and block her view from the window using an opaque window spray.
● Clean any spray-marked areas with an enzymatic cleaner, followed by a light spray of surgical spirit.
● Create a 'core area' where she feels secure, such as a spare room, and fill with her resources.
● Use a pheromone diffuser in the room to further increase security.
● Provide extra stimulation, such as play and activity feeding.
● If you catch her spraying, do not punish her as it will only make the problem worse.

50 Quick Fixes

15: Urinating on your bed

If your cat has urinated on your bed, it has not been done out of revenge because you've been out at work all day; it is the action of a nervous or insecure cat. She has reacted to your absence by seeking areas that smell most strongly of you. Urinating on it associates her smell with yours and is an attempt to increase her confidence whilst being home alone.

At all costs, do not punish her for this behavior. Punishment will make her more nervous and damage the bond you have with her. Be proactive by reviewing the type and locations of all current litter boxes – see Quick Fix 9, on page 74. Restrict access to your bedroom and consider leaving her in a smaller area of the house when you go to work; this should increase her sense of security.

16: Spraying on shopping bags

Most cats are not fazed by new items arriving in their homes, but to anxious or easily upset cats, the sudden appearance of a shopping bag can prove too much of a challenge. From your cat's point of view, her territory has changed, and the new items (bags) smell unfamiliar – they bring odours from external locations. As a result, she may spray on the shopping bags to reassure her that this, indeed, is still her territory. Try the following:

- Refrain from shouting at your cat as this will only compound the issue.
- Put your cat in another room and distract her with a toy or treat while you unpack the shopping.
- Discard the bags immediately.
- Try and make her feel more secure in her environment by providing high-up resting places and extra hiding places.
- Plug in a pheromone diffuser to ease insecurities.

17: Scratching the furniture

It is normal behaviour for a cat to scratch in order to sharpen her claws and mark her territory. However, scratching furniture is destructive and it is costly to replace the damaged goods. The key is to provide your cat with a more attractive alternative.

If she is reaching up and scratching on vertical surfaces, such as the side of the sofa, provide her with a vertical scratch post; it must be strong enough to withstand your cat's weight and tall enough for her to stand on her hind legs at full stretch.

If she is scratching on horizontal surfaces, provide a large flat corrugated cardboard scratcher – cats love cardboard! Place the new scratching post in a place where she spends lots of time, and reward her with a favourite treat each time she uses it.

18: Chewing wires

Cats chew wires and cables if they are bored or they are practising hunting prey. This behaviour is potentially fatal to your cat and dangerous to your home and family. The following suggestions should deter your cat from chewing wires:

- Close off rooms of particular interest to your cat.
- Secure electrical wires and cables so they are not dangling free.
- Hide exposed wires behind furniture or conceal them in electrical casing.
- Coat the cord in a disagreeable substance, such as bitter apple, to discourage biting.
- Provide alternative sources of stimulation, such as daily interactive play sessions and activity feeders to divert your cat's attention.
- Unplug all cables from the mains when they are not in use.

50 Quick Fixes

19: Climbing curtains

Cats are born climbers with a need to live in a three-dimensional world, and therefore must be able to access high places. Curtains and blinds provide cats with an opportunity to have fun, expend energy, and access those high-up resting places. However, this results in damage to your property and can also be dangerous for your cat.

To deter this curtain-climbing behaviour, you will need to provide your cat with an interesting alternative, such as a cat tree, or climbing frame. Place the new climbing frame near to the curtains as a reminder of where she should climb, and reward any advances towards the new frame.

20: Scratching wallpaper

Cats have a strong instinct to scratch. Outside, a cat can scratch gateposts, trees, and many other surfaces in order to sharpen her claws, but inside she may lack somewhere to do this.

To curtail your cat's wallpaper-stripping habit, you will need to provide an alternative scratching location. Place a large sisal scratching post in the area most targeted, and read 'Older cats and scratching' (page 31). Providing an outlet for her energies through play will stimulate her and distract her from the wallpaper. If you catch your cat scratching wallpaper, do not get angry with her – instead, distract her with a toy.

If all else fails, secure a sheet of hard plastic against the most targeted walls; this will soon stop the destruction.

21: Sitting on the computer

Does your cat like to sit on the keyboard when you are trying to type? Does she perch on the monitor and stalk the cursor? If so, then follow the handy tips below. They could prevent you from losing hours of unsaved work in the flick of a paw!

Prior to working on the computer, have a 15-minute play session with your cat, followed by a tasty protein treat. She will then be tired and contented, and likely to have a catnap.

To discourage her from napping on the keyboard, place a small cardboard box on or near the desk; cats love cardboard even more than they love you! To entice her into the box, place some tasty treats and an item of your used clothing inside.

Finally, if all else fails, keep your office door closed, and make it a no-cats-allowed zone.

22: Digging up flowerbeds

Digging is an important part of a cat's eliminative behaviour and, from a cat's perspective, your flowerbeds can be a very inviting alternative to their litter tray as the soft soil makes digging easier than with regular cat litter. However, many cat owners become very irritated when their plants are damaged as a result. Try the following to deter your cat from mining the flowerbeds:

● Cats find the scent of citrus offputting, so sprinkle lots of lemon and orange peel around your flowerbeds as a deterrent.
● Invest in a motion-activated sprinkler; this will spray a controlled jet of water as your cat approaches the 'forbidden' area.
● Encourage your cat to an area of the garden where she can toilet by providing a latrine, as follows. In a private area of the garden dig a hole (about 3ft/1m square) and fill it three-quarters full with gravel. Cover this with a thick layer of sand or soil and then add some cat-soiled litter there to encourage use. Clean the latrine regularly.

50 Quick Fixes

23: Jumping on kitchen surfaces

Cats jump on kitchen surfaces because they provide a high-up place, giving your cat security and a great view of her environment. They may also offer an added reward – tasty goodies! To deter this unhygienic habit, try the following:

● Be consistent on where your cat is allowed/not allowed to go, and never encourage your cat to jump up on surfaces.
● Make the kitchen surfaces as unpleasant for your cat as possible by putting double-sided sticky tape on the edges; cats hate sticky stuff on their paws and will soon learn not to jump up.
● Remove temptation – don't leave food out.
● Provide your cat with an acceptable high-up resting place, such as a cat tree; reward her with her favourite treat whenever she uses it.
● Tempt your cat up to the tree by leaving a sprinkling of catnip there along with some tasty treats.

24: Resistance to handling

If your cat was previously happy being picked up, but now shows a sudden avoidance, take her to the vet for a health check as a precaution. If she has never liked being handled, she may not have been socialized as a kitten, or she may have had bad experiences while being handled previously. You can help her to accept being held by doing the following exercises:

1 To begin to gain your cat's trust, stroke her when she's relaxed, and place your hand softly on her side for a short time. Offer her a treat for allowing this.
2 If she tolerates this, crouch down to her level and try picking her up a few inches from the ground (supporting her body and holding her close for security), then immediately put her back down. Reward her instantly.
3 Gradually increase the height you lift her and work up to being able to transport her to another room. Reward her each time with a tasty treat or some interactive playtime.

25: Biting hands during play

Young cats engage with their peers in rough-and-tumble play. If feline playmates are unavailable, cats may try to play similarly with people. Cats are attracted to anything that moves, and when your hands move during playtime, it is enough to stimulate the hunter in your cat, resulting in biting and scratching. This sort of play might seem harmless when she is a kitten, but can be dangerous if she bites you as an older cat. To stop your cat using your hands as a target, try the following:

● Avoid any games that involve directly using your hands. Instead, give your cat an acceptable outlet for her predatory play behaviour by providing fishing-rod toys. Engage in two 15-minute intense play sessions per day.
● If she does bite your hand, try to ignore it. Confrontational behaviour on your part will only make the problem worse.
● When your cat settles down, reward any calm behaviour with gentle strokes and a tasty treat.

26: Biting when being stroked

Some cats enjoy human contact, while others tolerate only small amounts before they let you know they've had enough – this is often referred to as a petting and biting syndrome. Cats who were not handled as kittens, or who were poorly socialized, are more likely to show this behaviour. It takes time and patience to increase your cat's tolerance of being petted and handled, so be sure to progress very slowly.

● Start by stroking her for very short sessions.
● Refrain from picking her up.
● Avoid touching sensitive areas, such as her stomach and legs.
● Watch her body language and stop petting before she attacks.
● Reward her with tasty treats.
● Allow her to escape if she wishes to do so.
● Gradually increase the session time.

50 Quick Fixes

27: Pouncing on people's feet

Cats that pounce on your feet are most often under-stimulated in their current environment. They need to play and to practise their hunting skills, and if they haven't got another outlet for this behaviour, then they will practise on you! Try the following tips:

● If she tries to attack your feet, distract her by throwing a toy in the opposite direction.
● Provide another outlet for this behaviour with interactive play sessions (see pages 42–43) and puzzle feeders (see page 49).
● Try to remain calm!

28: Doesn't want to play

Play is an essential activity for cats of all ages. It encourages bonding between you and your cat, it's mentally stimulating, prevents boredom, reduces anxiety, and is a great form of exercise. Some cats are born to play, but others need a little encouragement and motivation.

One way to motivate your cat is by providing her with the right toys. Cats are natural hunters, and although a toy may look like a mouse, it has to move like a mouse too, or your cat will generally ignore it. Cats like to hunt, stalk, and chase objects that are mobile. Toys that mimic prey-like behaviour will be more enticing to her and will create a high level of activity. Fishing-rod toys are excellent as they maintain constant movement, similar to the prey that she would be hunting in the wild.

If your cat doesn't seem to want to play, persevere and continue to encourage. Two intense play sessions daily would be ideal. Change the toys regularly, always supervise the play sessions, and make sure you end each game on a happy and positive note.

29: Rejecting a collar

Collars are potentially dangerous for cats, as they can easily become caught on something such as a branch or a fence. But if you do decide that your cat needs to wear a collar, for cat-flap access or identification purposes, use a quick-release collar which will quickly 'snap open' if she is ever caught up. To get her used to the collar:

- Collect some of her facial pheromones and rub on the collar.
- Place the collar on the floor and allow her to sniff it for a few days.
- When you first put the collar on, distract her with an interactive toy.
- Gradually increase the length of time she wears the collar.
- Be calm and patient and do not force her to wear the collar.

30: Rejecting a new bed

Is your cat refusing to sleep in her new bed, preferring your pile of ironing or a duvet instead? If so, a few persuasive measures can help change her mind.

The problem is not usually the bed itself, but its location. Try placing her new bed on top of a cupboard – cats prefer high, slightly hidden places. Heat is always tempting to a cat, so consider placing the bed above a radiator or buy a radiator bed.

Changing the bed's smell can help too. By adding an item of your used clothing, you will help surround her with the communal scent of the family and this will reassure her of her territory.

31: Aggression between cats

It is not unusual for the relationship between two cats that have coexisted happily together to suddenly break down for no apparent reason. If this occurs, it is important to pinpoint when their behaviour changed and what recent changes have occurred in the house. A new baby or pet, sudden changes in daily routines or house redecoration are all factors that can cause upset. Try the following to get the cats back on track:

● Seek your vet's advice to rule out any medical causes, such as pain.
● Separate the cats in the short-term and start their introductions over again (see pages 32–33 and 36–37).
● Take things slowly, at the cats' pace.
● If the reintroductions go well, gradually bring them back together in the house.

● Provide extra feeding stations, high-up resting places, hiding places and litter trays.
● Plug in a pheromone diffuser to reassure both cats that they are on safe territory.
● If you witness any friction, distract them with a toy. Do not be tempted to physically intervene during a fight, or you may get injured.
● Be patient and reward any good behaviour.

32: Fighting neighbouring cats

Cats are very territorial and defending their territory will often result in a fight which can become very intense and cause injury. If your cat gets into regular scuffles with neighbouring cats, you will need to intervene. Cat densities in towns are higher between dusk and dawn, so keep your cat indoors during these hours. Creating a 'time-share' arrangement with neighbouring cat owners could also help.

Construct high-up platforms, walkways, and hiding places in the garden to enable the cats to avoid one another. Discourage neighbouring cats from coming into your garden by setting up a motion-controlled sprinkler as an extra deterrent.

33: Attacking your new partner

Some people enter into an exciting new relationship, only to find their cat hates their new partner. Cats are very territorial and when feeling threatened, fearful, anxious, or confused, they tend to respond in the only way they know – by hissing, staring, and swiping. If your cat acts like this towards your new partner, try the following:

- Do not rush the introduction process; follow your cat's pace.
- Maintain your cat's usual routine.
- Ask your partner not to stare into your cat's eyes, or make any direct approach towards her – she will view this as threatening.
- Your partner should take over feeding duties and be the sole treat-giver; this will help to build positive associations.
- Ask your partner to play regularly with your cat to help them bond.
- If all else fails, your cat is telling you something: find a new partner!

34: Aggression towards owner

Your cat is sitting by a window and spots another cat outside. Suddenly, your cat becomes very agitated and hisses. You walk over to her to see what all the fuss is about and she unexpectedly launches an attack on you. This type of aggression is known as 'redirected' aggression. It occurs when a cat is unable to gain access to her primary source of agitation (the cat outside the window), so lashes out at whoever or whatever is nearest – you!

When cats react in this way, it is essential to handle them with caution. Your cat will be frustrated and highly aroused as she cannot get to the target. Do not attempt to handle her; give her space and allow her time to calm down from the provoking stimulus. If possible, close the curtains, turn the lights down, and allow her time to relax and recover. It may be worth planning ahead and putting a few environmental modifications in place to prevent this from happening. Try blocking out the window with opaque frosting until things have settled down.

35: Aggression between cats after vet trip

Taking a cat to the vet can cause problems upon her return if you have other cats. Her former friends may uncharacteristically attack her because, from a cat's perspective, her scent has changed and is now unrecognizable; the familiar communal household scent has been broken down. To prevent this from happening:

● Schedule routine veterinary visits for all cats simultaneously, so they will smell the same.
● If only one cat has an appointment, collect her facial pheromones on a cloth and store in a plastic bag. Repeat the process with the other cats. When your cat returns from the vet, keep her alone for a while. Gently wipe the cloths over her body to re-establish the family scent.
● When you eventually reintroduce the cats, monitor their behaviour and offer treats as a means of distraction if required.

36: Fear of the doorbell

Does your cat race out of sight each time the doorbell rings, only to be found hidden under a bed? Cats who have a lack of socialization or have had little experience of household noise can find unusual or loud noises particularly frightening. Here are a few tips to help desensitize her to the sound of the doorbell:

● Provide your cat with a 'safe room' away from the feared sound, where she can feel secure and relaxed.
● Ask a friend to come to the house and ring the doorbell at a pre-arranged time; make sure your cat is in her 'safe room' at that time.
● When the doorbell rings, play and reward your cat for calm, relaxed behaviour. Withdraw the attention as soon as the noise stops. You can do several short sessions throughout the day.
● After several sessions she will become more used to the doorbell; you can then try bringing her into a room closer to the sound.
● Reward calm behaviour. Over the course of many sessions, gradually decrease the distance between your cat and the sound.

37: Fear of a new baby

Cats are sensitive creatures and dislike change and disruption to their routine. Imagine how confusing it must be when a new baby is brought into the family home – there is suddenly a funny-smelling, strange-sounding creature on their territory. To ensure your cat and baby develop a good relationship, follow these tips:

- Maintain your cat's normal routine.
- Introduce her to the baby under supervision.
- Let her smell the new baby – praise and reward any calm behaviour.
- Do not restrain her; allow her to escape if she wants.
- Allow her to smell and explore the baby's belongings – she will soon realize that these don't pose any threat.
- Plug in a pheromone diffuser; this will provide extra reassurance.

38: Won't swallow a pill

Although some cats will readily swallow tablets, often medicating a cat can be a very difficult task. It is hard to convince a cat to do something that she doesn't like doing and to add insult to injury, many medications taste awful! The problem can be exacerbated if you also find the process daunting – the cat detects the tension in your muscles and your negative body language. Follow the guidelines below for some simple techniques for stress-free medicating:

- Take a deep breath and remain calm.
- Enlist the help of a family member if possible.
- Gently, but securely, wrap your cat in a towel or blanket.
- If using a liquid preparation, tilt your cat's head to one side, while carefully using a plastic dropper to administer the liquid.
- If the medication is in tablet form, use a pill-popper for ease.
- Gently massage your cat's throat to induce swallowing.
- Reward your cat with a tasty treat immediately afterwards, so she learns to associate the procedure with something nice.

50 Quick Fixes

39: When cats grieve

Cats, like humans, seem to go through a grieving process after another pet dies. If it was a close companion, your cat will be confused as to where the other cat has gone. As a result, she may seem anxious, more vocal, clingy, and perhaps will search from room to room for the other cat. To add to the grief, she sees her human family members upset, which further upsets her. Recognizing your cat's grief is the first stage to helping her.

Cats are creatures of habit, so try and keep her routine as normal as possible, including regular play, petting, and grooming sessions. You may be tempted to overcompensate with affection, but this won't work. Instead, make sure your cat is kept stimulated and when the time is right, perhaps consider adopting another pet (see pages 32–33 and 36–37), but don't rush into this; be guided by your cat.

40: Excessive self-grooming

It is quite normal for a cat to spend hours grooming herself but when the frequency and duration of the sessions increase, there is clearly something wrong. Excessive grooming can be the result of fleas or stress, or a sign of an underlying medical condition. It is therefore essential to first seek a vet's opinion.

If your cat is given a clean bill of health, overgrooming is likely to be a displacement behaviour caused by stress or conflict. Grooming is calming to a cat, so it may increase during challenging times such as the arrival of a new baby, or when overly bored.Interactive play sessions and extra attention can help counteract the stress by distracting her. Provide some high-up resting places and low-down boltholes to help her feel more secure again. Activity feeding will also help prevent boredom while you are out at work. If all else fails, ask your vet for a referral to a cat behaviourist.

41: Waking you up in the night

Unlike humans, cats sleep for long periods of the day and are most active between dusk and dawn, which is their instinctive hunting time. Typical complaints about a cat's nocturnal activities include vocalization, walking over sleeping owners, and damaging ornaments. Your cat is not deliberately trying to prevent you from sleeping, she just doesn't have an understanding of what time is socially acceptable for her natural behaviours! To help promote a good night's sleep for both you and your cat, try the following:

● Close your bedroom door and wear earplugs.
● Ignore her when she miaows, as this will only make matters worse.
● Have an intense play session with her just before bedtime, and then give her a tasty protein treat.
● Provide her with food puzzles – if she wakes in the night these will occupy her.
● Try keeping her awake and active during the daytime; she will be more inclined to sleep at night.
● Do not punish your cat as this will simply reinforce the behaviour.

42: Excessive vocalization

While some cats are naturally quiet and spend much of their day sleeping or grooming, others find it difficult to be quiet. If you are the owner of a Siamese or other Oriental breed, you will need to live with the noise, because these breeds are the most prone to this trait and you will not be able to change their behaviour. However, if your cat is not an Oriental breed and her incessant chatter is driving you to distraction, here are some things worth considering:

● If your cat has a sudden onset of vocalization, consult your veterinarian as this may be a health or age-related problem.
● Don't reward the miaowing. The most common cause of excessive vocalization is attention seeking. Cats learn to miaow when they want to be fed or to go out. Ignore her vocal demands.
● Reward quiet behaviour with a game or favourite treat.
● Enrich her environment – some cats that lack sufficient stimulation may vocalize out of boredom, so make sure you have regular interactive play sessions and provide activity feeding (see pages 42–43 and 48–49).

50 Quick Fixes

43: Eating woolly clothes

Eating wool or fabric may be a result of genetic predisposition (Siamese and Oriental breeds seem prone to it), early weaning, environmental triggers, stress, or boredom. However, it can be a serious problem, causing intestinal blockages. Try the following tips to help dissuade your cat:

● Prevent access to any targeted edible materials.
● Increase the level of stimulation and activity with interactive play and foraging opportunities.
● Apply a taste deterrent, such as menthol, to the fabric to discourage her from future nibbling.
● Increase the fibre content in your cat's diet.

44: Hiding under the bed

Easily worried or fearful cats may retreat to safe hiding places, such as under beds, if they feel threatened. If your cat has taken sanctuary under your bed, try the following to encourage her to come out:

● Provide her with alternative 'safe places', such as a cardboard box or a high-sided igloo bed; cats feel more secure if they can't be seen.
● Tempt her out with tasty treats, leaving them close to her hiding place if she refuses, then gradually increasing the distance.
● Play sessions with a fishing-rod toy are excellent for interacting with her or luring her out of hiding.
● When she finally appears, let her come to you in her own time.
● Never try to force her out from under the bed; this will increase her anxiety and make her more fearful.

45: Attention-seeking behaviour

Some cats are particularly needy for attention and their demands can get irritating, especially when they occur in the early hours of the morning. In order to prevent this behaviour, you must reward her when she is *not* engaging in attention-seeking behaviour – give her a tasty treat or cuddle when she's quiet. Cats love predictability and routine, so sticking to daily habits will not only help to reduce attention-seeking behaviour, but also help to build her confidence. Schedule grooming and cuddle times into her day and use interactive play and puzzle feeders to enrich her environment, so that you are not the only source of activity and entertainment.

46: Keeps going back to her old home

If you think that moving house is stressful for you, then think how your cat must feel. Cats are hugely territorial and dislike change. A new home will have different sounds and smells, which will make her feel anxious and insecure. If you have moved a short distance from your old home, your cat may take the opportunity to navigate back to her old, familiar home. If your cat has been wandering back to her old haunts, try the following:

● Keep her housebound for four to six weeks.
● Ask the new owner to act in an unfriendly way towards her if she returns.
● In her new home, set up a 'sanctuary' room with all her resources, and plug in a pheromone diffuser.
● After about a month, let her out for short supervised periods when she's hungry.
● Be calm and positive, and reward her each time she comes back to your call.

47: Refusing to return at bedtime

Are you having difficulty getting your cat in at bedtime? Being lively at night is normal for cats. However, if you would prefer your cat to be in the safety of her home at night, try the following:

● Provide her with a 'sanctuary' to which she will want to return.
● If you can train her to come when called (see page 27), bring her in at dusk and restrict her access to the outdoors until dawn.
● Produce her favourite cat food when she does come back.
● Reduce her need to hunt by using prey-like toys in play sessions.

48: Escaping from the garden

Cats instinctively like to wander, climb trees, and search for prey. However, the modern world can be very hazardous, with busy roads, unfriendly neighbouring cats, and the risk of theft and poisoning. By securing your garden, you will have the reassurance and peace of mind that she has the opportunity to be outside, while being safe and secure in your garden.

If you want to keep your cat in your garden, you will need to put up fencing of at least 6ft (180cm) in height, and covered in a fine wire mesh. It must have an inward-facing overhang (at about a 45° angle), to prevent your cat from climbing over the top. Make sure you enrich her garden environment by providing hiding places and sunbathing perches, and her own private latrine.

50 Quick Fixes

49: Hunting birds

A cat's prey drive is so strong that even the most well-fed cat will naturally enjoy hunting and capturing birds. However, many people, including cat owners, are concerned about the damaging effect this has on our wildlife population. Try the following to help protect our feathered friends:

● Fix several bells to your cat's collar – this may give her targets a little time to escape.
● Do not leave food for birds on the ground; provide them with a raised bird table.
● Keep your cat inside at dusk and dawn; these are the most important times for birds, because they feed then.
● Make sure your cat is well fed before she goes out. Try offering her some meat on the bone, as this will occupy her and leave her less time for hunting.
● Provide an outlet for your cat's hunting instincts by having several interactive play sessions, in which her hunting desires can be fulfilled without damaging wildlife.

50: Bringing prey into the house

Cats are first and foremost natural-born hunters, and when your cat leaves you a little 'present' in the form of a dead mouse or bird, she is expressing her natural role as a mother and teacher, bringing gifts in an effort to train and please you.

Although you may find this behaviour difficult to deal with, it is part of a cat's natural behavioural repertoire. Don't punish your cat, as she won't understand and it will only cause her anxiety. Instead, give her some affection and praise – after all, this is a special gift from a special friend! If your 'gift' is still alive, then quietly recapture it and return it to the wild. If your cat has got a high prey drive, schedule several interactive play sessions daily to satisfy her hunting desires.

Index

Index 95

Acknowledgements

Author's acknowledgements

I would like to express my sincere gratitude to those people who have helped, encouraged, and inspired me throughout the writing of this book.

Firstly, I would like to thank my editorial and design team, namely Trevor Davies, Tracy Killick, and Alice Bowden. Thank you for giving me the opportunity to write this book and for all your hard work in turning my words into this final product.

Thank you to all the wonderful cats (and owners) that I've worked with over the years; it's been a pleasure to be on this journey with you. Although we have sometimes met with challenging times, we always got there in the end!

A special heartfelt thanks goes to all my wonderful cats, past and present, especially my two current cats, Clicquot and GiGi. Thank you for all you have taught me about cat behaviour, and for providing me with many smiles and much laughter along the way.

Finally, this book would not have been possible without the support and encouragement of Lainey. Thanks for reading the many drafts of this book and correcting my copious 'Kim rambles', not to mention putting up with my incessant cat-chat over the years!

Publisher's acknowledgements

Thank you to the following people for giving their time and bringing along kittens and cats for the photoshoot: Sandra Strong of www.dogs-on-camera.com; Ros Karamath of Stepping Stones Cat Rescue (Stepping Stones Rescue/facebook); and the team at Fur 'n' Feathers Pet Shop, Streatham Vale, London. Thanks to our models Alison King, Sara Thomas, and our author Kim Houston. Thanks to Vicky and Maggie at Zownir Locations Ltd for providing a beautiful apartment for the photoshoot (www.zownirlocations.com). Thank you to Pets Corner (www.petscorner.co.uk) for their help with supplying props and petcare items. Thank you to Matt Hoskins for the use of the photographs of his cats (Furlined on Flickr). And lastly, many thanks to John Davis and his assistant Dave Foster for the photography.

Picture credits

Every effort has been made to contact copyright holders. However, the publishers will be glad to rectify in future editions any inadvertent omissions brought to their attention.

All photographs are by John Davis for Octopus Publishing Group Ltd, with the exception of the following additional material.

Alamy Juniors Bildarchiv 78a; Mauritius 80b
Fotolia Hetizia 4–5; Julia Mashkova 73a; maksymowicz 81a; Minou Amélie 79a; steheap 79b; Vera Kuttelvaserova 72a;
Getty Images Akimasa Harada 43b
Matt Hoskin/furlined/Flickr 32, 37ac, 54–55b, 66, 72b, 89a, 90
Shutterstock Alexander Kockin 75b; Alexey Savchuk 74b; Claudia Veja 80a; DavidTB 92; DigiCake 75a; GooDween13 91; Konstantin Sutyagin 47b; MaxyM 77a; Myroslava Pavlyk 76b; Noko3 71b; Ruslan Kokarev 93b; S J Allen 83a; Susan Schmitz 86a;Tony Campbell 85b; Veera 37al; Yala 70a
Thinkstock Acmanley 1; Andrey Shchekalev 3; BananaStock 29br; Chang Ching Hwong 76a; Elzbieta Sekowska 93a; Emily Skeels 89b; Feedough 77b; Frankiefotografie 12; James Berghout 47al; kimmik69 9l; Lulamej 73b; Mattia Pelizzari 71a; Micha Bednarek 68–9; Mitja Mladkovic 88a; Pavel Timofeyev 86b; Pyzata 22br; Rafal Olkis 82a; Velllena 47ar; Veryolive 2
Warren Photographic 85a

Editorial Director: **Trevor Davies**
Production Controller: **Sarah Connelly**
Picture Researcher: **Giulia Hetherington**

Produced for Octopus Publishing Group Ltd by Tracy Killick Art Direction and Design
Project Editor: **Sarah Tomley**
Editor: **Alice Bowden**
Art Director: **Tracy Killick**
Proof Reader: **Louise Abbott**
Indexer: **Hilary Bird**